WALKING WITH WHITE EAGLE
IN SACRED PLACES

A Library of the White Eagle Teaching

BEAUTIFUL ROAD HOME

THE BEST OF WHITE EAGLE

THE BOOK OF STAR LIGHT

CHAKRAS, AURAS, SUBTLE BODIES

EARTH HEALER

FIRST STEPS ON A SPIRITUAL PATH

FURTHER STEPS ON A SPIRITUAL PATH

A GUIDE TO LIVING WITH DEATH AND DYING

HEAL THYSELF

HEALING THE WORLD

INITIATIONS ON A SPIRITUAL PATH

JESUS, TEACHER AND HEALER

THE LIGHT BRINGER

THE LIVING WORD OF ST JOHN

PRAYER, MINDFULNESS AND INNER CHANGE

PRACTISING PEACE

THE QUIET MIND

SPIRITUAL UNFOLDMENT ONE

SPIRITUAL UNFOLDMENT TWO

SPIRITUAL UNFOLDMENT THREE

SPIRITUAL UNFOLDMENT FOUR

THE SOURCE OF ALL OUR STRENGTH

THE STILL VOICE

SUNRISE

TREASURES OF THE MASTER WITHIN

WALKING WITH THE ANGELS

THE WHITE EAGLE BOOK OF HEALING MEDITATIONS

WHITE EAGLE'S LITTLE BOOK OF ANGELS

WHITE EAGLE'S LITTLE BOOK OF COMFORT FOR THE BEREAVED

WHITE EAGLE'S LITTLE BOOK OF HEALING COMFORT

WHITE EAGLE ON FESTIVALS AND CELEBRATIONS

WHITE EAGLE ON THE GREAT SPIRIT

WHITE EAGLE ON DIVINE MOTHER, THE FEMININE AND THE MYSTERIES

WHITE EAGLE ON INTUITION AND INITIATION

WHITE EAGLE ON LIVING IN HARMONY WITH SPIRIT

Walking with White Eagle in Sacred Places

YOUR OWN
SPIRITUAL PILGRIMAGE

White Eagle

*with the Stories and Photographs of Pilgrims
and Drawings by Rosemary Young*

THE WHITE EAGLE PUBLISHING TRUST
LISS · HAMPSHIRE · ENGLAND
www.whiteaglepublishing.org

First published 2014

© Copyright, the White Eagle Publishing Trust, 2014
Drawings © Copyright Rosemary Young, 2014

British Library Cataloguing-in-Publication Data
A catalogue record for this book is available
from the British Library

ISBN 978-0-85487-233-6

*The publishers are most grateful to those who have
supplied accounts of their pilgrimages for this book, or
have provided the colour illustrations*

Set in 12 on 15 pt Baskerville at the Publishers
and printed in Great Britain by
the Halstan Printing Group, Amersham

CONTENTS

INTRODUCTION   *9*

PREPARATION FOR A JOURNEY   13

An Ancient Heritage   *15*
Your Personal Quest   *18*

PART ONE:

SEEKING THE SACRED PLACES   21

Places of Power   *25*
The Gift of Imagination   *30*
The Silence of Pilgrimage   *34*

PART TWO:

MAKING A PILGRIMAGE   39

Religious Pilgrimages   *41*
The Guiding Star   *43*
Getting Ready for a Pilgrimage   *44*
Your Preparations for Physical Pilgrimage   *45*
Inner Pilgrimages   *47*

How to Begin your Inner Pilgrimage   *49*

    1. Visiting a Place of Worship and Ritual   *52*

    2. A Visit to a Holy Master's Ashram   *53*

    3. Visiting a Well-known Sacred Site   *54*

      The Mountains of Tibet   *55*

      Visualization: Inside the Great Pyramind   *56*

      Visualization: the Path of the Labyrinth   *57*

My Own Physical Pilgrimages to Walk Labyrinths   *58*

Walking Meditations – Earth, Air Water, Fire   *62*

— Colour Section between pages 64 & 65 —

PART THREE:

MEMORABLE PILGRIMAGES   69

A Personal Search: the Himalaya   *69*

    A Personal Search: the Andes   *71*

    A Personal Search: Tibet   *72*

Dragon Hill, Berkshire, England   *74*

The English Downland   *77*

A Mountain in Southern France   *79*

The Stone Monuments of Britain   *82*

Wild Nature in Australia   *88*

    Wild Nature: the Great Barrier Reef   *90*

    Wild Nature: Uluru   *92*

The Labyrinth   *94*

    The Labyrinth: Chartres Cathedral   *94*

    The Labyrinth: White Eagle Land   *95*

    The Labyrinth: Lightning Ridge   *97*

Some Indiviual Tales of Pilgrimage   96
   Ephesus, Turkey   97
   Avebury (poem)   98
   The Pipes of Old: an Avebury Moment   99
   Newgrange, in County Meath, Ireland   101
   Iona, Scotland   102
   The Little Temple for World Peace, Sri Lanka 103
   Tintagel, Cornwall   104
   Rosslyn Chapel, Scotland   105
   Assisi, Italy   107
A Final Word   108

PART FOUR:

EXPLORING SACRED PLACES
WITH WHITE EAGLE

                                        111

The Quiet and Sacred Places   113
Inner Pilgrimage to the Mountaintops   115
Where Ceremonies have Taken Place   116
Deep Truths Written in the Stones   118
Stonehenge   120
An Inner Pilgrimage to Stonehenge   121
Avebury   122
Carnac, Brittany   123
America   124
Buildings of Heavenly Power   125
Glastonbury – and St Albans   126
Ancient Temple   128
Pyramids, Temples of Initiation   130
The Magic Island of Iona   132

Inner Pilgrimage to the Temple of Light   *134*
To Be a Pilgrim   *136*
Finding the Holy Grail   *137*

APPENDIX 1: The Tree of Light Breathing Routine   *139*
APPENDIX 2: Sacred Places Mentioned in this Book   *141*
   More Ideas   *144*
A NOTE ON THE ILLUSTRATIONS   *147*
   Colour Section   *147*
   Line Drawings in the Text   *148*

INDEX   *151*

INTRODUCTION

THE SPIRITUAL teacher White Eagle tells us of centres of power in our world, sacred places that once used remain irradiated with light and spiritual strength. As we unfold spiritually, we may become more aware of the mystical power held by these centres of light and their capacity to teach us. When we visit these sacred places we may receive spiritual guidance, arising from the power we experience there, and through making a pilgrimage to a sacred place we reconnect our busy, modern lives with the ancient wisdom. That ancient wisdom is, White Eagle would say, the information that forms part of the original blueprint of human life on the earth and underpins much of the world's religious and spiritual teaching.

White Eagle, who has used the mediumship of Grace Cooke to speak to us, describes himself also as spokesperson for a wiser Brotherhood in spirit, who help humanity to understand their true spiritual nature, and to grow in wise love for all life. Always encouraging, loving and strong, he is a friend to thousands of people all over the world and a spiritual guide to them in a path of gentle unfoldment.

Sacred places, he reminds us, occur all over the world. Our planet is plentifully endowed with beautiful and holy sites: some of religious significance and some of such beauty or majesty that they seem to have a holiness to them. Some have been created, apparently by human beings, in ages long past, while with others, such as high mountains, the very power of nature inspires awe and a sense of a greater life. Yet pilgrimage is an intensely personal thing: what is a place of pilgrimage for one person will not always resonate with another. We choose our locations for pilgrimage, and can plan our own journeys. One of the reasons for this book is to assist in that process.

There is never any reason to think, 'I don't live near anywhere sacred'. We all do. In the book THE LIGHT IN BRITAIN, Grace and Ivan Cooke, founders of the White Eagle Lodge, described a pilgrimage to spiritual sites in their own land, plus one in nearby Brittany. Their experiences at these sites inspired thousands of readers. Following their guiding light, yet not always their footsteps, this book intends to lead you, as a spiritual pilgrim, to have your own experiences, at whatever location you are drawn to. With White Eagle's guidance, you will be able to experience and discover your connection with different sacred places and maybe develop that into a full-scale pilgrimage.

After some prefatory words from White Eagle's teaching, this book is divided into four sections. In the first, 'Seeking the Sacred Places', White Eagle teaches of the ancient centres of power in the world and how their etheric traces remain sources of wisdom. He describes how we can prepare ourselves and make contact with the power of sacred places through finding the silence beneath the noise of everyday life and by using the power of imagination.

In the second section, 'Making a Pilgrimage', Jenny Dent gives practical advice on how to approach and plan a pilgrimage, whether it is in the physical body or through inner meditation. Jenny is Mother of the White Eagle Lodge, a position once held by her grandmother Grace Cooke, just mentioned.

In the third section, 'Memorable Pilgrimages', inspiring tales of real-life pilgrimage experiences offer examples of how significant a pilgrimage can be.

Finally, in the last section, 'Exploring Sacred Places with White Eagle', we return to teaching. In this part, White Eagle guides the reader by offering insights into the power of some ancient and sacred sites.

Occasionally White Eagle speaks of masonic symbolism, and this is to be seen in the context of ancient ritual, not modern masonry. Various such terms are clarified in the footnotes, and the appendices offer lists of places for those planning a pilgrimage as well as outlining the 'Tree of Light' breathing routine, which is mentioned a few times in the text. There is, of course, a vast literature on the places mentioned that cannot be summarized here, but among White Eagle Publishing Trust books we would recommend as further reading are:

THE LIGHT IN BRITAIN, by Grace and Ivan Cooke (1971: now out of print, but available from libraries).

WISDOM IN THE STARS, by Joan Hodgson (originally 1943, most recent edition 2005).

THE LIGHT BRINGER, by White Eagle (2001).

PREPARATION FOR A JOURNEY

A Sacred and Living Truth

K ING ARTHUR, the legends tell, dwelt in the West Country of Britain and gathered around him a number of knights. They were a brotherhood of chivalry and loyalty and courage. The story is told how, on their return from their long journeying, during which they had been tested for their purity and gentleness, strength, wisdom and love, these knights gathered at the Round Table, about which many a tale has gathered. At the centre of the Round Table was the symbol of the Holy Grail, offered to each knight on the return from his long quest. At this table of King Arthur a chair was left vacant, we are told, waiting for the coming of the pure and stainless one, the true initiate who alone can occupy that chair.

This story is considered to be, we were going to say, many hundreds of years old – but it is truly as old as the world itself and not confined to any period of a few centuries. It is certainly a symbolic story, but only in part, you may discover. Of course the outer mind will say 'a myth!' … 'a fairy tale!' – but even fairy tales have a foundation in truth.

Such stories of a long past are interesting and entertaining, but have they any relation to our own particular need, here and now? True, we can read many books about happenings in bygone days, and learn interesting things about Egypt, Greece or maybe Atlantis. It is not enough that you are told one or two details about a previous life or lives, interesting as they may be. You still want to learn how to interpret these happenings. Tales of Arthur seem today mere myths, and yet what we want to impress upon you is that behind these stories is a great spiritual and universal truth. You will find that such stories all have a simple and yet profound spiritual meaning.

If you study the myths of King Arthur and the knights of the Round Table, in these stories handed down to us by the ancients you may see enshrined, as we do, a wonderful and mystical truth. These same truths are embodied in your great literature and in noble art, for through the writer, the artist and the musician, the rays shine. They shine through scientist and through doctor, through all gifted souls who give forth true wisdom, knowledge, beauty, and well-being. The sacred mysteries – which in truth and fullness dwell deep within your own self – are revealed by the relics of legends, still telling of the great and holy human beings who brought sacred and living truth.

The wisdom brought to humanity so many years ago was never meant for the lips, rested on no authority and called for no priesthood, but dwelt in the heart. The secrets of the spirit cannot be conveyed by word of mouth. It is not possible to express in the written word those secret and inner mysteries of the past. Only when you meditate will you go to the higher planes, where you will probably see great and lovely things.

Unless you have keen spiritual insight these symbols will mean little. No one can teach you. You have to learn how to interpret the symbols yourselves; in other words you will have to learn the language of the spirit. You will have to learn this truth.

Truth lies within every soul. With each of you, your vision varies according to your evolution. You are under the wise guidance and direction of your Master.* We see the mysteries as a symmetrical and beautiful coloured-glass window, and we see the sunlight shining through them, producing gems of colour. One ray may glint through, picking up a purple hue, while another may shine through the golden glass, and others through the blue, the green, and the red. All the seven colours of your limited spectrum are there, and so the light of the ages shines through to humanity.

An Ancient Heritage

Let us turn to the mystery school said to have been established by King Arthur and his knights. Arthur, the grand mythical character of whom you read, was not of your own little time, not of your age, but was one of the kings of the ancient, ancient land. The story, on the outer plane, is that King Arthur was placed as a babe in the care of Merlin. If you know anything about the sage who is called Merlin, you will know that centuries ago he prophesied the future of humanity on this mystic isle to the secret brotherhood. He also said that within people dwelt a

*A Master is an extremely wise and illumined soul who, after many earth incarnations, has mastered all the lessons of physical life and continues to work closely with the earth vibrations to bring illumination and upliftment on the path of brotherhood and unconditional love.

divine power which would arise and open their eyes. The brotherhood established by King Arthur was of high degree. The preliminary work was done; circles or sanctified places of power were established.

For ages afterwards the earth elementals, the nature and air spirits and even the angels themselves have watched over these holy places, so that even those who are insensitive to spiritual things find themselves drawn there. The wise ones watch from afar the radiation of the power of each place, now affecting the lives of millions of younger brothers drawn thither, either physically or in thought, because of their reading and study. They think they go because the place is of historic interest or natural beauty, but we say that within each person who visits there is a quality that is attracted by and responds to the influence and the power of these magical places. I believe this very air, this atmosphere, this ether, is charged with sound waves, with vibrations of certain harmonies, inspired by a master musician and speaking to humanity of that wonderful mystery in tones of music. At such centres there is power concentrated, power which radiates and permeates into human life and human understanding. Buried still in those regions is ancient light and power that can only be released spiritually. The spirit of those great ones who first came to this ancient land still lingers.

Be true to this ancient light. Be true to your great heritage. Humanity has to stand in reverence and in obedience to that divine light, that divine urge. We must learn to apply that light before anything else in life, before everything that is done, individually or nationally or internationally. Then will the light and power imprisoned within the very

stones of the earth be released. Rise, put on your armour
of light and work for the coming of the new day! – not to
satisfy any personal ambition or desire but for the coming
of light and happiness and brotherhood to the land. Obey
the urge towards service in every detail of your life.

When you understand your great heritage, you arise in
the spirit of Christ – that is, in goodwill, justice, truth and
brotherhood. Be true to the light within your hearts, to the
light that is shining and has shone in the hearts and lives
of all those noble brothers, saints and teachers and servers
of the past. Rise in spirit and fight the battle of spirit over
darkness and despair, over the destruction of the lower
mind and the ugliness which now prevails on the physical
plane! Make your stand for truth, for beauty, for love and
for the great brotherhood of all life.

What do our words mean to you? Are they just words
and nothing more, or do they convey to you a fire of inspiration to go forth and seek and find, that you may be
initiated into the greater mysteries? It is time for you all to
understand the work that is now proceeding, the bringing
into manifestation from the very soil of your land the true
light of spiritual brotherhood: brotherhood in very truth,
not in word only but in life – in service, in kindness and
co-operation, in patience, tolerance and love.

Your Personal Quest

Remember how King Arthur directed his knights to go in search of the Holy Grail.* The knights of the Holy Grail go forth to gain experience and to search. The quest of humanity throughout the experiences of earth life is symbolized in that ancient quest. People search in many places for the inner secrets of life, the inner secrets of nature and for the heavenly mysteries, and in their hasty search they overlook the one place where the jewel lies.

Interpret that quest mystically. The soul goes forth in quest of the Holy Grail, of the light divine, which he or she knows exists somewhere. Do you know the meaning of the Grail? The Holy Grail is not in distant lands, nor in the heavenly spheres of life. The soul has to proceed onwards and not be lured away. It has to keep on keeping on in its search for the Holy Grail … and always finds that it lies deep within the cave of the soul, the heart centre. It is in the simple heart of humanity. That which led the candidate to the Holy Grail was first to open the light or love or kindliness within the heart to his or her fellow soul. Then and then only the light from above found entrance into the secret chamber, and guided them in their quest.

Your own story of King Arthur portrays the mystery, the story of the sacred heart, the inner mystery described as the quest for the Holy Grail. You have reached the

*Generally, a sacred dish or cup that is central to Arthurian legend and associated with the cup Jesus drank from at the Last Supper. Cathars (see pp. 65–8) linked it very strongly to the 'Holy Spirit' or 'Holy Ghost'.

point where you are awakened, or are awakening, to the consciousness of the universal purpose of life. Ever remember there are countless Holy Grails, and each one will eventually find their own. The key is there, and only there; through all the myths and the legends of the past, of all countries, is to be found this same truth. We reach that centre which always has been, always will be, world without end ... the centre of truth wherein we shall find the records of all that has ever been, and all that is.

Learn, my dear ones, that the calm, faithful heart, which rings true through every experience of life – in adversity and disappointment – this is the heart which is gaining admission into the mysteries of the Holy Grail. We would make absolutely clear the fact that you will not realize your goal through mental pursuit, through your mind, through your brain, but only in the innermost sanctuary of your spirit, of your heart. This means that by your life and aspirations and prayer, consciously or otherwise, you are seeking the Holy Grail.

You must prepare yourselves for this, must pray and seek. Follow the light as it breaks in your own heart; obey the voice of your inner spirit and do those things which you know are right. Follow this voice through your life and in every detail of the work that has been placed before you. The paths of humility, love, service, worship of the Creator, tolerance, faith, kindness – all these are paths which lead the soul towards the Holy Grail. As the soul searches truly for this prize, it learns the way to the place wherein the Grail Cup rests.

Remember: within is the true light which will lead you. You and every soul must find the heart, must enter the temple of the Rose Star* and alone and silently find the Holy Grail.

As you are raised in the consciousness of the temple, the light may illumine you and shine through you, opening your vision to the glorious truth, pure spirit, which is sometimes symbolized by the flashing jewel. You will see this jewel right in the centre of the blazing Star, and from that centre the flashing rays go forth. Hold this picture, this meditation. It will assist in the expansion of your aura, aid your spiritual development. The rays will reach up and out and down, and you yourself will merge into that flashing jewel, the diamond life. When a soul discovers this innermost treasure it is all aglow with power, with life, with supreme happiness and peace.

The power which is infinite fills you … and you are sent forth as a knight in the service of the Master.

*Symbolically, the Rose is the symbol of the heart and also of the creative inner peace wherein the Star, which here represents spirit, is born. The Temple of the Rose Star is a temple of brotherhood but also somewhere wherein this miracle of creation may be regarded as happening.

PART ONE

Seeking the Sacred Places

CENTRES of power exist. They exist in every continent. God-beings have lived and worked in many parts, and left reservoirs of spiritual power to which those of the light are drawn to continue their work. They have formed magnetic centres into which are poured from time to time cosmic and planetary forces, which in turn help to keep the equilibrium of human evolution.

There are many centres of power, many places that have received concentrated rays of God power. At present there is so little known of the ancient religions, and the power centres which were established all over the earth in ancient times. The mystery schools* established in the beginning have continued throughout the world's history, spreading to one continent after another. Inscriptions still testifying to the existence of these schools can be found on relics of stone, but the modern investigator does not yet comprehend their meaning.

*There are known examples of mystery schools around the eastern Mediterranean in the centuries before Jesus, but as White Eagle uses the word we might consider the mystery school as a 'spiritual university' of the ancient wisdom truths of eternal life, and also extending to spiritual science and arts, including such subjects as astrology, sacred geometry and the science of healing.

We want to tell you about the mystic isle of Britain, which is a jewel set in the silver sea. There are some exceedingly beautiful centres of spiritual light in Britain. There are other centres in Europe, in the Middle East, in Egypt, in the Far East, in America, in the Pacific – indeed, all over the world. These are places where the rays of light have been concentrated for a period of time, and in such places you will feel greater force. As surely as the sun's rays penetrate the earth and all physical matter, so the light of the ancient wisdom still impregnates the stones and the earth about them.

In these centres the forces are just there until the ring or the magic is broken or dispersed. Time does not exist in the spirit world. When you come into the world of spirit you will notice in these places complete silence and stillness.

Those drawn to such places have already learned certain inner truths that abide, because while the physical life passes, the inner wisdom once learned from a mystery school is never lost. That is why many of you feel the stirring – the ancient wisdom – within your breast. You are able to feel the power which has been gathered in certain places. You do not need to be convinced, because you have once seen into the invisible world, and you know.

You will come to learn much more than you know at present about the ancient races and ancient lands – but only when you have developed your own power to receive impressions from the ether will you read the true ancient history of buildings and stones. The written word can prove helpful to a certain extent; but wisdom lies beneath the veil. Thus many have written what they feel to be a true record of those happenings, and yet humanity is ever confronted with conflicting stories. On the surface this must be so, but the one who seeks within his or her own centre will read beneath the myths, the symbols, and allegories of the past, that truth which is eternal ... changeless. To this centre we must ever journey, if we would learn wisdom. So in these stories handed down to us by the ancients, we see enshrined a wonderful and mystical truth.

Read, meditate – and when I say 'read' I do not mean read books necessarily, but learn from observation and the universal life. Then you will understand these sacred mysteries which in truth and fullness dwell deep within your own self, and yet are revealed in the relics of legends still telling of the great and holy ones who brought sacred and living truth. Their names die out, their memories pass away; but about the places where their feet have trod, where brave hearts once beat and brave hands were wrought for God, there clings an aura of sanctity and power which is an everlasting heritage.

With the passage of years truth can become obscured; there is a curtain pulled down by the wise ones. The preliminary work was done; circles or sanctified places of power had been established. The wise ones watch from afar the radiation of the power of each place, now affecting the lives of millions of younger brothers drawn thither, either physically or in thought, because of reading and study. At such centres there is power concentrated that radiates and permeates into human life, human understanding.

You may, very soon if not now, see an increase of light and spiritual realization in your beloved land, for it is an age-old heritage. It is the work of the brotherhood in spirit today* to release this ancient light, still imprisoned both within the earth and within all men and women. There will be established once again, all over the earth, these mighty magnetic points. As those living in the physical life have their vision unfolded they will see in your beautiful land the rising of the white light, and it will penetrate all life on this material plane. When this light, this truth, is released, a life more beautiful than any known on earth for many thousands of years will come again.

May this be a message to you of hope and inspiration. There lies before you a quest. You must take the road alone, every one of you. No one can travel for you and hand you the treasure. Pilgrims in the far-off ages were instructed by the God-beings. You must travel that road yourself. You must take the key from the inner recesses of your heart and unlock the door for yourself.

Although you travel alone, you are not alone, for all the other knights are travelling too, in search of the same treasure. You can comfort yourselves with this thought, that all travel the selfsame road, all meet the same obstacles, all go through the same fires. So, though you seem to travel alone, you are never alone, and in time you will en-

---

*The term 'brotherhood' is used to identify a group of spiritually aware souls working with a common purpose to help uplift the world. The terms 'White Brotherhood' and 'Star Brotherhood' are interchangeable, but in the context of the White Eagle work there is a particular awareness of a Star Brotherhood who use the symbol of a six-pointed star as a focal point for prayer and healing. Brotherhood in itself might be defined as the bonding of the soul with another (or others) in recognition and for dshared spiritual endeavour.

ter through the golden gate, the royal arch, into the kingdom of heaven, as surely as the dawn follows the night.

Do not let the world and the darkness of the unevolved hold you down. Go forward like pilgrims. Be pilgrims on this path of spiritual unfoldment.

Places of Power

All that ever has been, still is. All that has once been manifested remains, not perhaps in outer manifestation but on the inner planes. Every event in history, from a vast dim past to this present day, is impressed upon the ether. These records are known as the akashic records – the etheric records of the life of this planet. These records of the ages speak to the wise, the just and the true, to the masters of the wisdom, to those who have traversed the path of light and become initiates of the secret mysteries.

All that the world contains is first born from the invisible, and comes through into physical, or outer manifestation; and thus the mysteries of life were recorded, even before they were manifest on earth. Behind every manifestation in physical matter there exists both on the etheric and on the higher planes – astral, mental, and spiritual – a corresponding vibration of life. Such records are imprinted on the ether, and are the etheric or akashic records. These etheric records are within your reach.

Think of it! You have great libraries on earth which are said to contain the material records of all known events and all known races and their habits of life and their religions. All these records you have, but they are merely earthly records and incomplete indeed compared with the wonders of the akasha. These etheric impressions are never lost. When you have grown in understanding, you will find instantly any record you wish, of past lives, past histories of peoples and their religions – all the records of every book written, of every picture painted, of all music, however grand, however simple. Not only the works of the Masters are available, but all works into which the soul of humanity has been woven.

Only when the soul has awakened is it able to read them, however. Human beings have arrived at a point on the evolutionary path where they are ready to advance still further. So this knowledge, although it is still sacred and secret, is being given to true seekers, who are humble and pure in heart.

Your every life, your every past incarnation, is imprinted on the akashic record. This is why you yourself in meditation may rise for a moment to that level of consciousness where you can receive an impression of that past of yours. Sometimes such vision comes only vaguely. In the same way many people experience a feeling when they are visiting a supposedly strange place, or places that they have been to before. A vague shadowy something makes them say, 'This place is familiar to me'. People who remember in this fashion touch their akashic record for a flash. But such understanding comes only to the higher mind, to the son of God within the true seeker.

As you proceed on the path of inner unfoldment you will become more sensitive to the vibrations of the past experiences stored away in your soul. The higher etheric or soul body is a creation, not of physical birth, and not of eternity perhaps, but of long ages past. In this soul body we find woven the experiences of the past, the higher worlds, the higher planes of being. Those vibrations create pictures in mind or soul of scenes of your past.

In the halls of learning in the spirit world it is the usual procedure to throw upon an etheric screen scenes of past events, culled either from the life of some particular pupil or – should it be for a class or group – from scenes in the world's history. They may be scenes unrecorded on earth except to those who have an inner knowledge, records which are left impressed on the ethers of the earth. I cannot begin to give you a list of all the wonders of this invisible world, this great akashic record, that exist through the ages.

Those of you who have read about the ancient civilizations and what are now lost continents regard these conditions and places which once existed on the earth plane as now extinct. Yet all records of ancient races, their ceremonies, achievements and ritual remain. Great cataclysms – why have they been? Continents that seem to have vanished from the face of the earth still exist on the etheric planes, and past lives which we have once lived are not past lives at all. They are still ever present, as many of you can testify. Life as you once knew it on any of the lost continents or in ancient civilizations still is.

All is a question of your realization of the spiritual eternity. The sensitive, walking on holy ground and stilling the outer mind, opens a consciousness which is without limit or space. In spirit there is no time limit because all time is at this instant – in this instant we are in eternity. All that was or is to be is now. Thus you can go forward or you can go backward in time. That which in you is attuned to those ancient places can find its level. The soul can become conqueror, or master, of time; for it there is no time. It stands within the consciousness of eternity, and it knows truth.

If you know how to touch the correct vibration, you can tune into places that are thought to have vanished for ever. You can go back and instantly re-live any life or part of any life of your past, because past and present are all bound up together and inseparable, and their impressions are all there in the ether and can be tapped and seen at any moment in our meditations.

Great ceremonies have been enacted in places that now lie in ruins. Those of you who are developing this inner vision – but it must be pure and must be directed by the truth and the wisdom of God – see their ceremonies, see their mode of life. If you visit these places you will see these things for yourselves. Those ceremonies still live in the ether and can be seen by people with developed clairvoyance. Not only are the ceremonies to be seen but the actual people, the priests, often return to places where once they lived. It is one of the laws that people may return to places in which they have done special and great work.

You can, if you concentrate and give all your simple faith to the work, become en rapport with the etheric plane. It is an unspeakable power that you can contact and in a flash become part of, in full consciousness, if you work as you are advised. When you meditate, if you are working correctly, you will be only conscious of those more beautiful and harmonious conditions of life; these you will be able to see and hear and feel and smell with your etheric senses. Now remember that in meditation you are not only thinking or contemplating abstractly; you are creating with your higher mind a condition of life in which you are at that moment living and participating. The beginning of this stimulation lies in prayer and meditation, which, as we have already told you, means quiet, rhythmic breathing, a stilling of the outer mind, a going into the inner earth. The way to open the vision and awaken the consciousness is through quiet meditation.

By meditation we do not mean sitting down and either letting your mind run riot or trying to think only about certain things. By meditation we mean a going beneath all thought to the level of spiritual life, and becoming aware of the light. This is the light of the spirit. You will discover by this one true method what is undiscoverable merely by excavation, or by mind or brain study. The brain will carry you only so far, my children, and there it stops. It cannot penetrate further. You have to go beyond the brain into the etheric world. You have to train your own etheric mind to penetrate that world. Then you will see the mysteries of that world's past revealed in much the same way as by television. People will someday develop themselves as an instrument of this nature. Even there they will not stop, for still greater heights remain to be climbed and grander visions to be seen.

Do not be daunted, for as you reach the top of one mountain you will surely see a whole new range before you. As you press forward, your way will become lighter and more joyous, and life will only reveal more grandeur, more beauty and a deeper satisfaction, deeper happiness, deeper love for the Creator of all worlds and all systems; and for the Creator of the beauty and ecstasy, indeed the glory of one simple spirit – your own. You are but as a grain of sand upon a vast shore, yet God has given you individuality and divine intelligence nonetheless, has given you the power to comprehend the glory of the whole universe.

The Gift of Imagination

Normally you are conscious of the physical aspect of life; you study nature in the insect, the animal, the bird life, and the flowers, the bushes and trees; you enjoy the countryside, breathe the air, watch the beautiful sunset and are enthralled by the forms of the clouds – but you give no thought to that which animates these glories of creation. The normal person sees just the physical manifestation of life, and thinks of creation as subject to certain laws – which of course it is. But they ignore the intelligence behind the form, the beauty which brings to them so much joy.

Many are so accustomed to the everyday material

world that it sometimes seems incredible that any other life than this can be. They travel, conscious only of things of the material plane. They visit an interesting and historical building and pass onwards thinking little more about it. They may go to some hilltop or mountain in a remote district and breathe in the sweetness of the air. If they are sensitive, they feel something very beautiful and even realize, 'Why, this must be holy ground!'. The thought just flits through the mind and is gone. 'Imagination', they decide later. Yet imagination is truly the doorway to all the creative powers. It is a spiritual thing and opens up a higher world.

These people will take a country walk, and see very little. They stay unaware of the beauties of nature. They have not reflected their surroundings. For another soul will take that same walk and will become aware of maybe a thousand little details apparent to them in the hedgerow and fields, in the bird life: in the sunlight, in the shadow and in the atmosphere. Many details they will note. This soul is not merely observant with the physical eye, but with the spiritual eye also. Conceive a third one taking that same walk. This person has become more sensitive still to the spiritual life behind the physical form, and its sight again has greatly increased. This third person will not only see all the details of a physical nature, but also become aware of the pulsation or vibration of life and great beauty which permeates the physical manifestation. The soul of this person will reflect the spirit world.

It is important that we all recognize the value of imagination. The creative power called imagination is humanity's greatest gift. For if a man or woman were bereft of the power to create mind-images there would be very little left for them. We tell you most earnestly that true and real imagination is the doorway into the etheric world, the doorway into the higher mental world – and beyond that, into the celestial or heavenly world, and even beyond again into the cosmic world.

Most human beings draw a heavy curtain between themselves and the real world of spirit. Yet many people know that within themselves lie these spiritual forces. There is always an intuitive power telling you that you are spirit, and that there are unknown, untried, undeveloped forces within you. Do not be content just to listen to our words or to read the writings of the initiates and mystics and sages! You will never find what your soul seeks through reading books, unless your spirit is awakened or quickened. Seek truth for yourselves, and you will surely find the jewel, a treasure of great price. The spirit is supreme!

Have you ever thought that your whole life is directed, your every action urged through your mental images? You have to imagine your clothing, your house, your food, your everything before you can bring it into being. Your every activity has first to become in your imagination. Where there is no vision (or power of imagination) the people perish. They must indeed perish. What is vital is that your aspiration must grow Godward; all your imagining must be pure, beautiful and Godlike. God is beauty; God creates beauty; God has created you; and through you, God's creation, beauty must become manifest.

Do you see? I will try to give you an illustration. Let us consider the inner consciousness. Those who can respond to the finer vibrations of the astral world know that it is not merely thought which links you with the spirit world, but rather a feeling, a realization, or a vibration of the soul. The spirit world is not a place outside your present world. Some conceive the spirit world as being in the planes surrounding the earth, and indeed you are told this is so. And yet we come and say that the spirit world is within you. How are we going to connect the two ideas of the spirit world, at once as a plane of life outside the physical and as one contained within the soul?

Open your vision, yourselves. You must do this. Draw aside the curtain which is now before your vision and see into the life on the higher dimension. There you will see the beauty, the loveliness, the glory of that life, which is there waiting for you to enter; and you have the power to penetrate that veil and to serve from that level of consciousness. Keep up: look up. *I, if I be lifted up, will raise all men unto me.* If the Christ within you be raised up you will raise all who come within the compass of your spiritual vibration or radiation – all who witness your etheric, your emotional, your mental, your spiritual glory.

I want you to close your eyes and turn your thoughts inward. We can be aware of a plane of consciousness within which is dull and dark; or we can increase our awareness to a finer, quicker vibration, and become conscious of a matching sphere of life. As our thoughts become more beautiful, so the light within appears to grow brighter. If our thoughts remain ugly and dull, so the world remains drab and ugly. So we find that the world of spirit is reflected within the mirror of our own soul.

Leave the outer world and come into the inner world

of reality. As soon as you have learnt to attune yourself to it you are in it. It is all around you. Ponder, meditate upon this power. Train your minds. If you will daily endeavour to develop the inner consciousness, the inner life, you will find it so easy to go into our world of spirit. You will become acquainted with – no, you will be – the companions of the angelic brotherhood, who are ready to lift the veil and show you the very deepest secrets of nature and of creation, and of the life-forces in the earth, in the rocks, in the water, in the fire, in the air.

Do not think of the celestial sphere as far away from you. You are learning to register truth. You learn to penetrate the material aspect, and contact the eternal things.

The Silence of Pilgrimage

Pilgrimage does not involve withdrawing from society. Instead, we have to learn to contact the centre of stillness while we are in the midst of the throng. Imagine visiting a sacred monument, queuing to get in, and standing amid crowds of jostling tourists. We have to learn to get beneath all sound; we have to learn to become attuned and active in the deep silence, for that silence is power.

In the world, on the earth plane, life is noise, rush. There is no peace. The spiritual power is being dissipated. People may go to church, but there is very little silence even in the church; there is babble, not perhaps from physical talking, but more from mental talking. We can enter a place of worship on the earth plane and find it full of busy thoughts, and these are very noisy sometimes.

In past days people recognized the need for withdrawal from the outer world. They built temples of stone, which stood for the unshakable indestructible power of the spirit, wherein they worshipped their Creator. There in silence they worshipped the rising sun and made obeisance to the setting sun, for the light was the source of life and without the light there could be no life on earth. The vast concourse of people stood in silence with upraised arms to welcome the sunrise, and with the coming of the sun came also the spiritual power of their lives. In the older days also, in monastery and temple, there were long periods of silence and of physical aloneness, when we were separated from our brothers for many hours, so that we might have time for reflection and meditation.

Would that men and women would seek the silence more often, as we used to do in past ages! Even when we met in large numbers we worshipped in the silence. Even in our Indian days we, who had the welfare of the people at heart, used to repair to the mountains, climbing quite high to sit in meditation watching the rising and the setting of the sun, and we would not leave our post until we had an answer to our prayer. We did not attempt to solve our problems in the noise of the camp-life, but repaired to the mountaintop – the mountain of the higher consciousness as well as the physical mountain. There were great things accomplished in those days, things beyond the power of people today. Today the physical body so much has to remain in the outer world … in action.

Let us incline our eyes and hearts again unto the hills, from whence comes light, and where we can again become alone with ourselves. For we are seeking straightness of vision, wholeness, some measure of wisdom. Our human structure so quickly and easily gets broken down in towns. But once out in the open, say on the blessed downlands of England, we can breathe in the awareness of expanse, and our little beings can reach towards infinity. They can inhale truth concerning ourselves and all the deeper issues of being.

Of old, the student withdrew, quietly pursued the path, worked diligently, gave healing to the sick and comfort to those who mourned. Powers came which enabled the student to draw aside the veil between his or her world and the invisible worlds. These same powers can be yours today.

In this day of life, particularly in the Western world, there is little time for reflection and meditation, and yet the same law applies as in the old days of the monastery and the temple. We have said that usually communion (or communication) comes to those who have prepared themselves by retiring to a sanctuary or to the heights, but it does not always follow that you need seek to be alone in a church or sanctuary. Vision is one thing, but the act of becoming is through ordinary life – that course is set for you that you may learn the secret of being: and the secret is found through the heart, through loving. The very act of prayer truly causes a man or woman to 'plug in' to the world of spirit, to create the necessary conditions or spiritual state which enables him or her to hear the voice or message of the spirit. A world of unfolding beauty will open when you take the trouble to tread the path, proceeding by the way of meditation, prayer, devotion; not by ostracising yourself from life, but by living in the world as a conscious son or daughter of God. You must literally go forth to the battlefield of life, and there learn to discriminate between the false and the true, the real and the unreal.

The spiritual pilgrim must learn to reach deeper. The disciple has to learn to withdraw into the silence of his or her own lodge, which is the true inner self; there he or she has to seek solitude, and has to meditate and ponder on the spirit which is within. Not easy – oh, we know it ... it is not easy! 'Silence' does not mean necessarily absence of physical sound. It means the silence of all your vehicles: the silence of the physical so that it becomes as nothing; the stillness of the emotions, the stillness of the mental body and the silence of the spirit. In the brotherhood above there is no need for speech and even the thoughts are stilled. There is only silence, for it is only in the silence that the voice of truth is heard.

You are learning to seek the place of silence. In this silence is heard the music of God's voice; the truth that you seek is here, all truth, age-old truth. Do your best to preserve the holiness, the silence, the stillness. Noise breaks up the power. You build it up, we build it just like a fountain of light – and then the noise from the outer world, or the noise of movement and chatter, breaks it down and it just falls down as though you turned off a switch. You know, if you have a fountain in your garden and you switch on the electricity, the water comes up and spreads its cleansing properties all around, but if you switch it off it just goes down back again into its source. This is what can happen with spiritual power, with healing power. It is all built up by your love, your heart, and the angels, and if worldly noise is allowed to enter in, it goes back down again to its source. In the deep, deep silence we find God: not in the mind, not in great activity; but when all is still and a great peace is upon us.

Sit in the silence and you will hear secrets whispered to you. Go out on the sunlit downs with the sea rolling upon the shore beneath you, and listen with your heart.... You will hear secrets whispered to you. You will know how things happen, why things happen and how evolution is proceeding. And you will know where the key to the gate of heaven is to be found; you will know how to insert that key and unlock the gates. You will understand the meaning of every ceremony and every symbol that you encounter in the temple of the holy rites. All this you will know and you will understand the inner sacred meaning of the consecration of love, and you will experience the consummation of real love. You will follow the one path, my brethren: the path of real living, of the real expression of all the gifts which God has implanted in your body and mind and soul.

The key of this kingdom, as we have told you many times, lies hidden within the recesses of the human heart. The key to the mysteries of heaven, to the mysteries of life, lies in the heart, and the soul goes forth to search, search. These mysteries shall be no longer mysteries.

PART TWO

Making a Pilgrimage

Jenny Dent

A S WHITE EAGLE says in the passage, 'A sacred and living truth', at the beginning of this book, the story of the knights going forth in quest of the Holy Grail can be interpreted mystically as describing the journey of every soul. It is a familiar story throughout myth and history, one of spiritual progress. John Bunyan's PILGRIM'S PROGRESS is a different allegorical story of the same journey. The pilgrim, 'Christian', encounters many experiences on his journey which are symbolic of every soul's passage through physical incarnation.

Today, a spiritual pilgrimage is a ritual journey with a beautiful purpose. Much more than an ordinary trip for pleasure, the journey is filled with symbol and meaning; every step, every new horizon has significance. The pilgrim knows that the challenges which arise on the journey may change his or her life. New understanding and fresh inspiration comes. Memories, both joyous and painful, are explored, resolved and healed. A pilgrimage is not a holiday; it is a rite of passage during which significant inner transformation takes place. After the pilgrimage, your eyes are opened. You see the world differently.

Our busy, everyday lives are filled with moments of beauty that are often overlooked, and meaningful travel, such as the process of pilgrimage, illuminates those moments. Through the exploration of sacred places we are able to uncover deep inner meanings. With intentionality, the outer action of our journey of pilgrimage can be filled with inner meaning.

In some ways our whole life on earth is a 'pilgrimage', although many people are unaware of theirs. As spiritual pilgrims, we are all seeking throughout our lives. We all follow a path of spiritual pilgrimage, overcoming obstacles and moving towards our goal as we travel.

Spiritual pilgrims have many different reasons for choosing to journey:

- *Some are seeking inspiration and clarity.*
- *Some want a new vision, a change of mind.*
- *Some search for their spiritual paths.*
- *Some are deeply questioning their life's meaning.*
- *Some are committed to the idea and practice of pilgrimage.*
- *Some don't know why they are making a pilgrimage, but are following their feelings and intuition in setting out on one.*
- *Some want the time and space to concentrate on a religious path.*
- *Some seek harmony with nature.*
- *Some are spiritual adventurers, or like to travel.*
- *Some want to calm their minds and find peace.*

You may want to ask yourself, 'Why am I seeking pilgrimage?'

Religious Pilgrimages

Making a journey with religious purpose has been part of history for thousands of years. Many lands have ancient 'pilgrim' ways spanning hundreds or even thousands of miles. Pilgrimage is a part of most religions as it is traditional to attach spiritual importance to particular sacred places. Thus Tibetan Buddhists may trek until they can circle Mt Kailas, Muslims seek their Mecca and Christians their Jerusalem. Hindus may go to Varanasi (Benares), and so on. All these religions have their individual traditions, and local ones, too: sacred pathways and places of sanctity that their followers aspire to visit. Pilgrimage is becoming more popular, with, I have read, two hundred million people visiting the thirty-nine most popular sacred sites on the planet.

Some are shared sites. For example, what in Britain we think of as the Holy Land is a place of pilgrimage for Judaism, Christianity and Islam. The city of Jerusalem has been fought over so many times and was the focus of the Crusades. Yet the word 'Jerusalem' has become synonymous with the whole concept of the perfect city of God and 'the new Jerusalem' with a golden age of brotherhood.

There is a long history of Christian pilgrimage. Traditional places of pilgrimage are to sites associated with the life of Jesus. Pilgrimages are also made to Rome and to sites associated with saints and martyrs, such as the route of Santiago de Compostela. Similarly, Buddhists make pilgrimages to sites associated with the life of the Buddha. Hindu pilgrimages are also associated with events from the lives of various gods, with many sacred cities, rivers, lakes and mountains. Pilgrimage is even more important to Islam: the pilgrimage to Mecca is one of the Five Pillars of the religion and should be attempted at least once by all able-bodied Muslims. And in this way the tradition and ritual of pilgrimage is a familiar part of religious life all around the world.

To those following an individual spiritual path, the only rules and guidelines are those that come from deep within ourselves, from the light that guides us. This makes pilgrimage an exciting and empowering prospect, a journey of discovery and enlightenment to places that are uniquely personal to us. Have you always wished to visit a particular holy place? Do you have a personal 'Mecca' drawing you? Are you always making excuses for are not actually setting off to your Jerusalem? Or perhaps you live somewhere near a sacred or spiritual place but have never taken the time to visit it?

This book is intended to open up the possibilities for you. For maybe now, as you read this, the time has come to set aside the doubts and fears, the excuse about dependants or the lack of time or money. Every problem can be surmounted 'when the time has come' if you are clear and focused and set your will in accord with the divine will – the peace of God shining in your heart and through you.

It is good to remember that actually a pilgrimage is not really about 'getting there'; it is much more about all that happens along the way. It is about the tests and tribulations; the triumphs and so called 'failures'; it is about the 'downs' as much as the 'ups'. Remember, too, that quite often the arrival itself can feel like an anticlimax, and that it is only afterwards that the full significance of the journey becomes apparent. You may end up thinking you would never do it again, and yet know that what you did was absolutely part of your life's path; or it may become part of your way of living, to go on such trips, as it became for me. I found that it is as the pilgrim reflects on notes, experiences, meditations, contacts made during the journey, in the weeks and months that follow, that many realizations dawn.

The Guiding Star

Traditionally ancient mariners and travellers used the stars to guide their journeys. In the White Eagle work the symbol of the shining six-pointed Star is offered to students as an inspirational focus of guidance in many different ways. Among these it can help attunement to the individual's own 'guide' or wise inner companion. There are several references to the Star in this book: always, it should be considered as something that leads us on, just like the Star of Bethlehem led the Wise Men to the birthplace of Jesus.

It can do more than guide you onwards. White Eagle once spoke about its meaning in some profound words.

> *'What is the Star? We could never define it if we talked the whole length of an incarnation, but to sum up we would say that the Star is God's plan for humanity. The Star is the Creator's plan for the liberation of humanity. It is the symbol of creation; and in the very centre of the Star you will find eternity.'*

Getting Ready for a Pilgrimage

A pilgrimage can be an actual physical journey, or an inner spiritual journey, or both. Whatever its form, the preparation time is important. Plan your journey as carefully as you can. Make space in your busy life for the whole journey – that is, the experience that begins the day you conceive it. You may like to begin by actually writing down what your goals are for making the journey – why you are going and what you hope to achieve. Later, you may add to that list.

Sometimes the unexpected aspects of a physical pilgrimage are the physical problems that stand in your way (some of the stories that follow illustrate this – for instance, the one on p. 102). Places of pilgrimage tend to be either remote and difficult to reach, or extremely popular with other visitors. In both cases, be aware that the challenge of making the spiritual connection is an integral part of the experience of pilgrimage. Early pilgrims dealt with physical hardship, and certain places of pilgrimage involve great physical testing for us too. Sometimes this can be difficult to cope with, but remember that the 'earthing experience' of the physical struggle can connect us more powerfully with the land, the stones, the hills and the ancient power within them, however weary we feel! In popular places the challenge is different. It can be frustrating to try and fail to make a spiritual connection in a location heaving with tourists. We may long to get away from them, and yet they are everywhere. Opposite are some suggestions for coping with this challenge.

Your Preparations for Physical Pilgrimage

1.   Before entering the sacred place, centre yourself and imagine yourself 'under the Star' – that is, become very conscious of your own sense of being. An alternative is the 'Tree of Light' breathing routine given in the Appendix, p. 139. Ask/make the intention that if it is meant to be, you will find yourself alone for a few minutes to meditate quietly. Often this will happen as if by magic.

2.   When in the sacred place, don't rush, even if others are rushing. Walk quietly, trying to avoid your self-control being swept away by the urgency of other visitors. Don't rush to have a spiritual experience, just allow impressions to filter slowly through your consciousness. Your special experience may be to notice the lame dog by the track or the person in need whom everyone else has rushed past. Train yourself to just BE…. That is, inwardly open to the vibration of the place you are visiting physically (it is just the same if you are doing this journey only in your 'body of light' – see p. 47). Focusing the thought on the powerful symbol of the six-pointed Star helps the aspirant to do just that, inasmuch as it is an eternal, age-old symbol depicting through the interlocking triangles heaven and earth interpenetrating.

3.   Try to keep all your inner senses open and alert. When it feels right, look for somewhere to sit down on your own. Seek out quiet places off the beaten track. It is surprising how in the most popular of sacred locations you can often find an obscure chapel or a quiet piece of grass or a shady tree just outside: a little place where there is extraordinary power and contact, as if the power can linger there more easily. Of course, despite your best efforts, in public buildings it

can be hard to find quiet, and the experience of a physical vis-it may be disappointing because of outward chatter and dis-turbance from others – even friends. This is one reason why – having made the physical contact – a later inner follow-up visit can prove more uplifting. Sometimes, after a visit in the hurly-burly of the day you can go back quietly in the evening and meditate, even outside a door that is by now closed. If there is outer noise that cannot be avoided, embrace the happiness others are experiencing and use the awareness of that to help you 'tune in' even more at the inner level. Attunement comes far more easily in moments of harmony than when you are fighting conditions you cannot change.

4.   To open yourself spiritually, absolute stillness of thought and emotions is required. However important ab-sence of noise and 'busyness' at the outer level may seem, even more important is the stilled mind and gentle warm emotion of the spiritual seeker. It is also necessary to let go inner eagerness to achieve an experience. You may find you can visualize a bubble or shield of light surrounding you, shutting out the noise and disruption of other people. Im-agine the spiritual energies shining effortlessly through this shield like particles of light but filtering out the noise and chaos without denying it

5.   Having thus prepared, and sitting in a quiet space or walking around, think of and visualize the Star and affirm, 'I open myself to the spiritual power in this place'. As far as possible, leave your expectations behind. Don't be distracted by thoughts of 'seeing'. 'Feeling' is the way; trying to see can lead to disappointment Try to let go of ideas about what you expect to experience or find – be open to the unexpected.

6.   Be patient and don't try too hard – it can take time and gets easier with practice. If you can go several times to

a special place, it will be much easier to feel things.

7.   Lastly, don't carry any more 'baggage' than you feel you have to. That might be distractions like your feelings for other people, but also includes attachments to physical comforts and manifestations of modern life that run counter to the simplicity of the place. St Francis lived very simply indeed, and so did Buddha and Jesus; none of the builders of Stonehenge had cameras! Attune yourself as best you can.

Inner Pilgrimages

A unique part of the White Eagle path lies in the way his philosophy offers all of us the opportunity to make an inner pilgrimage, even if physical (geographical) movement is not an option, for whatever reason. White Eagle teaches all his students how to make inner journeys in their 'body of light', unrestricted by material circumstances or physical conditions. The body of light is the spiritual counterpart of the physical body. It could also be described as the intangible extension of the heart centre that we can project to any place or part of the universe to experience something which is out of the body's reach at that moment. The White Eagle teaching thus brings a whole new dimension to the concept of spiritual pilgrimages. We find:

- *that our journeys are not confined to the physical body;*
- *that the time pressures of life are no limitation;*
- *that geographical distance is of no consequence;*
- *that the experience can, with practice, be fully as memorable as a physical 'trek' to the chosen place;*
- *that physical restriction, disability, material ties or lack of resources do not inhibit our soul's ability for 'wingless flight'.*

Every one of us can learn how to use our 'body of light' to travel anywhere we wish. A significant part of White Eagle's work is indeed to encourage us all that even if outer journeys are not possible, we can become proficient in travelling in our 'body of light', both to physical places – and, of course, also in spiritual realms. It makes for a much more 'green' pilgrimage if you do it this way, as inner travel cannot damage the earth's resources or make you part of the invasion of some long-peaceful site!

Opposite is a guide to the 'wingless flight' you may make in your body of light, and below is some guidance in White Eagle's own words.

> *'A White Brother can move without limitation or hindrance. A White Brother can commune with his brethren and with the universal spirit of life and move into the world of spirit and commune with spirit, and bring back the consciousness of the experiences into the physical life. What is inspiration but the result of a memory of these spiritual journeys into the heavens?'*

How to Begin your Inner Pilgrimage

Begin your preparation for pilgrimage with the image of the Star. Imagine it shining just above you, shedding rays of light that illuminate your pathway and lead you to your place of pilgrimage. Use your breathing to help you become very still and poised and aware of the inner flame of light in your own personal sacred place, the inner temple of your own being. In this inner space it is much easier to feel the presence of your own 'guide'. Just as on other journeys or pilgrimages people may be led by a guide, so any inner journey can be clearly guided to avoid too many unnecessary 'detours'. If there is conscious awareness, the guidance obviously will be stronger and clearer. This inner guidance aids both inner and outer pilgrimages.

Your 'Wingless Flight'

1. In your quiet, prepared state of consciousness, speak inwardly with your guide. Ask to be taken in your body of light to your chosen place of pilgrimage. It may help if you have a picture or photograph as a focus for meditation.

2. Use your creative imagination! Imagine yourself arriving at the threshold or gateway of your chosen place.

3. Wait a while there ... constantly consider ALL your senses, not only inner sight. Here are some thoughts on how they may be used.

- *Smell*
Concentrate first on the inner sense of smell. White Eagle

reminds us that this sense is linked to the Earth element. As you think about the destination of your pilgrimage, what can you smell? Heavenly incense? The burning of sage in the huge vats in Barkhor Square in Lhasa, Tibet? The smell of the animals in the stable at Bethlehem? The most subtle perfume of a master?

*   *Sounds*

Now the sense of hearing. White Eagle reminds us this sense is linked to the Air element. Can you open your inner ears? As with all inner senses, begin with using creative imagination. Imagine the sound you might be hearing if you were physically at that place. The time will come when it will not be imagination: you will really be there.

*   *Taste*

Now taste! This sense is linked to the Water element. So now imagine what you might eat/drink on your pilgrimage. Or, maybe you are offered refreshment at a place of rest on your journey.

*   *Sight*

This sense is linked to the Fire element. After the previous 'creative imagination exercise' you will probably find that visualization and 'inner seeing' flow more easily.

*   *Feeling*

This fifth sense is linked to Ether, which is the vibration we contact behind all the inner senses. So, if you feel you 'have not got very far' with the other senses, now just rest with feeling and the sense of touch ... see what unfolds.

4. Now, enter/walk towards/explore/wander/experience the place of pilgrimage.

5. Find a place to sit inwardly, where you can become

absolutely still in every way. Let your intention be no thought – just to be. It may help you do this if you visualize being at an inner shrine on which a light burns…. Just be with that inner flame.

6. When you are ready, ask your guide to 'lead you back'. Use gentle breathing. Try to breathe back deliberately into your physical mind and emotions. You can retain the inner memory of your experience while re-emerging on the outer level.

7. As soon as you can, write down all you can remember, or put it into some sort of drawing or even a collage of writing and drawing – whatever you feel drawn to do.

8. Return to the experience whenever you wish. One of the special things about these inner journeys is that you can return often – not just 'once in a lifetime', and probably you will find that on each return, more will unfold. Obviously, the more you put into words and drawings, the easier will be your recall of it.

At the end of your inner journey, write down anything that felt more than just fancy and wishful thinking, particularly any symbol, or words. Later, as you reflect on these, more of their significance may be revealed to you.

Guided Visualizations

To get you into practice, overleaf are some guided visualizations you can use to prepare for your pilgrimage – physically or in thought.

1. *Visiting a Place of Worship and Ritual*

Cathedrals and ancient temples have often been built lovingly but as a statement of power too – the power of God and the power of the hierarchy over the ordinary people. For all this, the very grandeur of the building and its architectural beauty can touch and uplift the human spirit to heavenly awareness. For instance, when buildings are constructed with dimensions according to the principle of the 'golden mean', they can truly 'sing a note or symphony of divine harmony'. In addition the service, music and ritual used in these buildings over a period of time draws to that place great devas – angels of ritual and power.

Preparation

Visualize yourself approaching the building (be it cathedral, mosque or temple – one you know, one you would like to visit, or one you are preparing to visit), maybe looking at a picture or creating it in your mind's eye. Prepare with relaxed breathing and a prayer in your heart and to your own spiritual teacher and companion at your side. Ask that you may be open to the experiences visiting this place will bring you.

After asking for help, the next step is to surrender any desire you have for a particular experience. Just relax and open your heart; try to be present in your higher mind. You may like to use the six-pointed Star symbol as a focal point to help in this. Then, in your 'body of light', in your imagination, walk slowly through the building 'breathing in its atmosphere'.

Finally, in the outer or inner stillness, make a conscious effort to open yourself to the great devas of ritual and power, the angels of music and ceremony, those who have worked and worshipped in this place in days gone by. Maybe past-life memories will come; maybe nothing…. If it is nothing, try to surrender it back to the great body of life and remember that using your 'body of light' you can return any time – this does not have to be a 'once in a lifetime' visit!

After any 'visit', make notes in your meditation journal to review later as further realizations often come long after the initial contact is made.

2. A Visit to a Holy Master's Ashram, High on a Mountain Plain or Hilltop

Climb (in your 'body of light' if you are doing this at home) to a sacred hilltop place where there is maybe a small chapel or tor (a rocky outcrop on the top of a hill) or another physical building. Find a secluded comfortable place to sit and attune with quiet breathing and prayerful aspiration and begin your meditation….

If there is no building, imagine something very simple – like a little white Grecian temple or just an entrance to a cave in the mountain- or hillside. Inside there is only a simple, stone altar upon which burns a small oil lamp. The holy teacher greets you silently and you sit on a stone bench. No word is spoken; you bathe in the aura of the holy teacher, breathe in his or her qualities of love and wisdom. Whatever quality you need to take back into your physical life is given to you now.

Open yourself to absorb fully this opportunity for spiritual enlightenment and inspiration.

3. Visiting a Well-known Sacred Site

For many, the dream of a physical visit to one of the sacred centres of the world is a dream long held. Even if you cannot travel there physically (for whatever reason) come now in your imagination....

The Mountains of Tibet

Here it feels easy to 'touch heaven'. For those who are attuned, the Masters are indeed close and so are the great devas of the air.... The inner spiritual heart can be felt strongly and clearly in the wide, open spaces of the vast plateaux and glorious mountains. The clarity of the mountains and very high altitude seem to induce a spiritual feeling quite naturally.

Come with me now on an inner journey into the mountains.... Breathe in the clear air. Open yourself, as I do now, to the great angelic beings all around. I do not think I have ever seen such extraordinarily clear and yet muted colours. I am truly there. In the stillness an inner awareness may come to you of God's presence, the almighty power behind and within all creation. With your inner ears you may hear the great AUM – the note of God, of absolute harmony. There is a divine plan, divine order behind all life. Outwardly things may seem in disorder and chaos but inwardly there is a great stillness, the peace of utter surrender to the Creator.

Visualization: The Temple at Edfu in Egypt

Stand in thought above the grand entranceway. The winged disc crowns the great stone pillars. Horus guards the outer courtyard. With inner ears open you hear the chanting as you tune into a Temple ceremony from days gone by. With your spiritual guide and companions you join the Temple procession, walking nine times around the outer courtyard: three times three. Then the two priestly figures leading the procession, holding up the grand ceremonial ankh (symbol of eternal life) and scarab (symbol of the creator imprisoned in matter), enter under the winged disc and proceed through. You are part of the procession.

It comes now to the central point of the Temple. All wait under the grand columns as the priest and priestess proceed forward into the inner sanctuary wherein lies the great crystal in the form of a dodecahedron, symbol of the perfected soul. A great light shines from within the crystal as the ceremony proceeds. A beam of light reaches from the crystal to each participant as the priest touches it with the ankh. There then breaks forth a glorious sound of praise as the chanting rises to a grand crescendo. After a while the sounds die away and all is still....

Visualization: Inside the Great Pyramid

All is still here too: all is dark. It is warm in the innermost depths of the great pyramid of Giza – warm but not frightening or oppressive. A great sense of calm enfolds you. Rest in the womb of the pyramid, as though enfolded in the arms of Isis, the great mother of all life. In the peace of this special moment the inner mystery of birth into eternal life may be revealed to you.... Memories may stir in your higher consciousness of encounters with the master teacher dwelling within this pyramid, the great Master Hermes, the one known as thrice-blessed.

Open your inner awareness to him as he comes to you now. His presence floods this inner secret chamber with glorious golden light (almost blinding after the darkness). The light blesses and uplifts you. It shines into every cell of your being – a heavenly transfiguration.

Visualization: the Path of the Labyrinth

Walking a labyrinth can be like a small, symbolic pilgrimage. A labyrinth, as I use the word here, is a two- or three-dimensional form that is designed to have a specific purpose, which is to guide a soul on its journey to deeper understanding of truth. A maze to me is different: it is random, confusing. Unlike a maze, a labyrinth has a single, non-branching path to the centre, meaning you are not designed to get lost. It is designed in an elaborate structure or pattern. There are many sacred labyrinths around the world, and they can be a most helpful spiritual aid as we seek to follow a path of unfoldment or simply to understand and come to terms with all the stresses and complexities of our lives in this busy modern world. To walk a labyrinth is to explore your whole life in miniature.

White Eagle teaches that it is a fundamental aspect of spiritual law that we are given freewill choice over all the major events in our life. We make these choices before the moment of our rebirth when, with the help of our guides, we set up a 'life plan'. Hidden within this overall choice, and the destiny we have accepted in the context of our karma, there can be many twists and turns. It may feel sometimes as though we have taken 'a wrong turning' and gone backwards; it may seem we are at a dead end or stuck in a maze – a randomized pattern from which we cannot escape! If your life feels a bit like this right now, don't forget your guide and the shining Pole Star above, leading you forward on your pathway, in which the twists and turns are all part of the plan!

CHARTRES LABYRINTH

After opening with attunement to the Star and Star breathing, I visualize myself going to the glorious cathedral of Chartres, so beautifully placed on a hilltop in the old quarter of the city, with views over the surrounding countryside. I see the sun shining on newly cleaned stonework and marvel inwardly at the artistry and skill of the stonemasons of medieval times. Then I enter the dark nave, symbolically placing my right foot first.

For a moment, it feels as though I am stepping back in time into 'dark ages' now past, remembering karma I have since transcended. It must feel like this sometimes when we leave our heavenly life and take on again a physical body.

Then I tune in to the presence of my guide at my side. I feel her warm handgrip leading me forward. I enter the labyrinth. Each inner meditative journey is a little different. Allow yours to unfold with your guide's help* as you step forward under the Star. Maybe you reach the central six-petalled 'rose'.

In your meditation, sometimes you will reach this point and sometimes not. Sometimes the careful pattern of the labyrinth seems just a maze of confusion. But your guide is at your side, and will always lead you onward. Sometimes, in this visualization, I stop for a contemplation and meditative instruction from my guide on the way, and I always keep my labyrinth journal at my side and make notes of the realizations which come. Every inner journey is different, but all reinforce my awareness of the interpenetration of heaven and earth. Quite often I have an experience of being lifted up into a heavenly cathedral of infinite beauty and grandeur.

*A guide is a wise soul, not currently in physical incarnation, who has accepted the role of protection and gentle guidance to help the incarnated soul (with whom there is a strong bond of love and friendship) to face and accept all the challenges and opportunities chosen for that lifetime.

My Own Physical Pilgrimages to Labyrinths

At times I have walked two very different labyrinths, both inwardly and physically. I had long heard of and read about the famous one at Chartres Cathedral. I looked forward to my visit there with eager anticipation, and was dismayed to find on my arrival that I had come 'on the wrong day'! The labyrinth was covered with chairs. At present, these are only cleared back on Fridays.

But was it the 'wrong' day? White Eagle tells us 'nothing happens out of order or by chance'. I sat on one of the chairs in the nave, to meditate instead of walk. During the meditation I had on my actual visit, I found it very difficult to 'get anywhere' – I felt stuck, frustrated. Yet later I purchased a large picture of the labyrinth in the cathedral shop and have used it often as a focus for an inner journey there. It was precisely this experience that led me to the realization that an inner pilgrimage can be as meaningful and inspiring as a physical one.

I have also walked an outdoor physical labyrinth, many times. In the grounds of the White Eagle Retreat Center and Temple at Montgomery, Texas, USA, there is a very beautiful labyrinth made to a design quite different from the one at Chartres. This one, the inspiration of Jane Sorbi, leader of the White Eagle work in the Americas, is spiral in form. Different designs of labyrinths may help a student or spiritual pilgrim in different ways. This labyrinth offers those walking on it (or meditating by it) the opportunity to find deeper understanding of many aspects of spiritual truth. There is a particular opportunity to gain a deeper understanding of the mystic symbol of the rose blooming at the centre of the equal-sided cross of the elements. Moreover, as one walks the seven rings of the spiral, the opportunity arises to learn more of the mystic significance of the seven rays, through the symbolism of the spiral itself.

One magical sunrise, I had a very beautiful experience at this site. As I prepared to enter the spiral of the labyrinth, the rising Sun's first rays were shining directly across one of the arms of the cross to form a pathway of rosy sunlight to the central 'rose' of the labyrinth. It was fortunate that some inner prompting had also made me take my camera with me. The walking meditation practice which follows is one which came to me on this and subsequent visits. It brought back memories of my time in Lhasa, Tibet, perambulating around the prayer wheels in the Jokhang Temple precinct and walking seven times around the Barkhor Square.

The Montgomery labyrinth is designed to encourage a deeper understanding of the four elements, and at the centre point of the spiral, each element is depicted in different coloured stones. I began my walking meditation by focusing on fire and its soul lesson of love. As I followed the spiral path inwards to the central rose, I chanted 'AUM MANI PADME HUM' quite quickly and rhythmically, in time with my steps, as I had done in Lhasa when I joined hundreds of pilgrims, turning the prayer wheels as we went.

When I reached the central point, I took seven breaths. On the inbreath, and using the corresponding 'Tree of Light' movement, I visualized drawing down the light and love of God into the heart of the earth through the central rose of the labyrinth cross. Then as I walked the spiral outwards (this time chanting simply 'AUM'), I focused on the earth element and its soul lesson of service. At the end of the spiral, this time I did the outward movements of the Tree of Light, breathing the light up from the heart of the earth, through the connection of my feet and body with the earth. I then breathed it out in service to the world.

Next I repeated the inward walking process but this time focused on the air element. I went again to the centre of the spiral, and there, again using the Tree of Light routine, I visualized the light of the Star in the heavens being drawn right into the earth and to all the creatures of the earth, fostering the sense of the brotherhood of all life. On the final outward walk of the spiral, with each 'AUM' I breathed forth peace and focused on the water element, and back at the entrance to the labyrinth I concluded with the outward movement of the Tree of Light, still breathing out peace.

Walking Meditations – Earth, Air, Water, Fire

There are many ways to do a walking meditation but the most helpful writer is the Vietnamese Buddhist, Thich Nhat Hanh. You can do it quite simply, though, just using your steady pace to keep your mind focused and not too cerebral. A walking meditation is an ideal time to attune to the elements – not just in their outer manifestation in the physical world, but also at an inner level. White Eagle teaches that deep spiritual lessons are linked with each element. Thus:

The Fire Signs (Aries, Leo, Sagittarius) ...

... are linked to the lesson of LOVE

The Earth Signs (Taurus, Virgo, Capricorn) ...

... to the lesson of SERVICE

The Air Signs (Gemini, Libra, Aquarius) ...

... to the lesson of BROTHERHOOD

The Water Signs (Cancer, Scorpio, Pisces) ...

... to the lesson of PEACE

The individual's zodiacal Sun sign at birth indicates the main soul lesson for that lifetime. In accordance with this, and having discovered your Sun sign if you need to, begin your walking meditation by reflecting on its soul lesson. I recommend Joan Hodgson's WISDOM IN THE STARS for a full explanation of the soul lessons. Do some deep 'Star breathing'* and possibly, if in appropriate circumstances, use the Tree of Light routine (see Appendix, p. 139).

Then set off on an inner or outer walk, keeping 'conscious' all the time. As far as you possibly can, focus on all you can see, hear, smell, touch and even taste. Bring your outer and inner senses to life. Wake them up! Often we go around with our senses only half functioning, as we are so busy with cerebral things. Watch, observe, be 'mindful' of everything, staying with each sensation and really observing what new thoughts and feelings the sense impressions generate.

Despite my encouragement to be alert, remember that your impressions upon waking from sleep may also

*Linking visualization of a shining six-pointed Star with the in-and-out rhythm of the breath, for instance breathing out stress and worry; breathing in peace; then breathing in God's healing light and breathing that light out into the physical world.

be helpful. Here's a story from my own expereince to illustrate this. I visited the grounds of the now privately-owned Place Manor in Cornwall in 2011 (it was once an Augustinian Priory) to experience the immense peace of this corner of land. It was so peaceful that I lay on the grass and slept – awakening with a most harmonious feeling that lasted for the rest of the day. I could visualize carts of tin ore coming down the lane to the cove jetty and Jesus waving farewell to the ship's crew, vowing to return to be collected next year. It left me certain that Jesus was (and is – in his body of light) still in this magical, mystical part of South West England.

Take a notebook with you to jot everything down for later reflection, or if you do not want to break your concentration, make your notes the moment you finish your walk. As a way of keeping the mind focused and random thoughts at bay, it can also be very helpful to use appropriate affirmations as you walk. For example:

'I am at one with the earth and the world of nature.'

'I breathe in the life of the earth.'

'The power of nature fills me and flows through me.'

GETTING THERE

STANDING STONES

TO THE QUIET PLACES

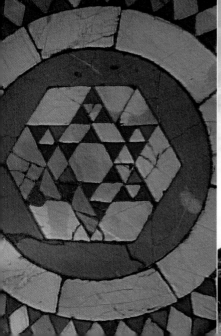

THE LABYRINTH
EXPERIENCE

CATHAR
COUNTRY

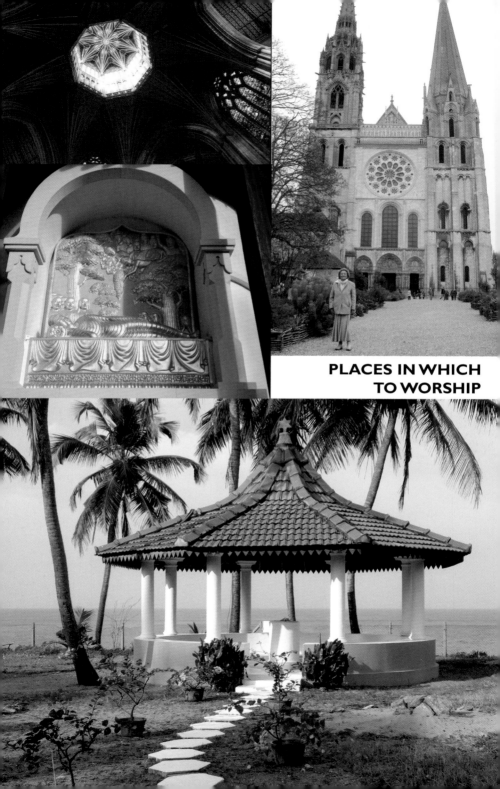

PLACES IN WHICH TO WORSHIP

PART THREE

Memorable Pilgrimages

A PILGRIMAGE can be a life-changing spiritual experience, sometimes in a way you are not anticipating. For example Grace Cooke, White Eagle's medium, was invited in 1931 to join a party from the French Polaire Brotherhood, to travel to the region of the river Ariège, just north of the Pyrenees and in southern France. They went in order to make a connection at the château of Lordat with the energy or power left there by the persecuted Albigenses or Cathars of the thirteenth century.* Notionally, but probably not in fact, their task was (with her mediumistic guidance) to seek buried treasure that had been left there. None was found, and yet she writes:

'During our stay we climbed each morning to the summit of the mountain (Lordat was a little village high up in the mountainside, and the castle stood above it) in the hope of being led to the right spot for beginning excavations.

'From the beginning we were strongly impressed by

---

*'Cathars' and 'Albigenses' are two names used by their detractors for the opponents of the Catholic Church in mediaeval times, principally but by no means exclusively in Southern France. White Eagle describes them as a brotherhood, and part of one that forms part of a continuous line from ancient times to the present day.

the dual nature of the unseen powers around us. There were times when the dark forces were predominant. Then … [there] came, like a breath of heaven, a sweet, pure, gentle, loving influence like a spiritual illumination, which made us certain of the presence of immortal brothers waiting and watching. At such times as these we felt we were under the protection of great white wings, guarded by a power which must be experienced to be believed…. We were constantly reminded, by the whispers of the unseen … that Christ is all-love and his spirit has power to comfort and protect from all harm. This strengthened our will to proceed. Many times this wave of spiritual light and power caused the dark veil between matter and the inner world to become thin, to such a degree that we found ourselves in company with the gentle spirits of the Albigenses, who for centuries had walked this very plateau on which we stood.

'On the third day after our arrival, when we were idly contemplating the grand panorama of mountains under the intensely blue sky with, in the distance [the path winding away towards] the ancient castle of Montségur, my attention was caught by the sudden appearance of a shining form…. "Shining" is the only word to describe the aura of the spirit who appeared, but his manner was as normal as that of any human being might be who, while out walking, had stumbled by chance upon a stranger. He appeared simple, kindly, and treated the situation as naturally as if it were customary for discarnate people to talk to men and women. He looked like an old man at first sight; that is to say, he wore a longish white beard and his hair was silver, but apart from this his skin was youthful and clear, as though a light shone behind the flesh, and his warm blue eyes were alight with an inner fire. He was clothed in white, in the garb of some early order of Christian Brothers and bore himself with noble meekness. "Could this be one of the Albigenses?" I asked mentally. Yes. It was true; by sign and symbol he proved to me that he belonged to this age-old Brotherhood. Why had he appeared in this manner?'

'He indicated that he had come to help in the search. However, he said that no material treasure would be found until men were ready to use it, until they had found the spiritual treasure, which was the secret of how their own lower nature could be transformed – the base metal turned into living gold. He indicated that in the life and teachings of Jesus the Christ would be found the key to this spiritual treasure. He spoke of John, the disciple beloved of the Master; how he had not died "as most men die" but had passed onwards to a higher life in a body of light as his Master had done before him. He had remained on earth for a very long time, travelling to the East and to the West, coming indeed to this very place where he had meditated and communed with his Master. He spoke of the inner mystical teaching from the Master which he, John, had passed on to his followers and which had been handed down through secret brotherhoods through the centuries, and that this mystical Gospel was in fact the source and secret of the treasure of the Albigenses.

[The story is continued by Ylana Hayward]

'After the visitor had withdrawn into the inner world from which he had come Mrs. Cooke "seemed to live in

a haze of happiness for days". She said years later that
the experience remained one of the most vivid and memorable of her life. "Words could not describe", she says,
"the sweet and wonderful love of this simple Brother". As
for the Polaires' treasure, none was ever discovered. The
expedition was ill-equipped for such a venture. At last the
task was abandoned, and to all appearances the attempt
had been useless and the message of the Sages falsified.

'But had it? It was as if the contact with that pure and
great brother who had come, she felt, from what she called
"the sphere of St John", had brought about a permanent
change of consciousness in the medium, so that thereaf-
ter her life's work began to take form. Teaching began to
come through her from the world of spirit, through her
guide White Eagle, that gradually formed the philosophy
of love that has helped and healed souls all over the world,
and, in White Eagle's words, "helped the light in the heart
grow" in thousands of lives. The teaching has become a
simple revelation of mystical Christianity, which at the
same time, transcending the limits of dogma, seemed quietly to bring the wisdom of the East and West together.'

A Personal Search

When a pilgrimage is meant to happen for a spiritual purpose, quite often events 'fall into place' to allow it to happen. Jenny Dent here writes of the pilgrimage experiences
that have inspired her spiritual work.

A Personal Search: the Himalayas

'On my first trek in the Himalayas I had my first glimpse
of the mountain which has come to mean so much to me
– Machapuchare. I knew I had to go back there to spend
more time in the aura of this beautiful mountain, which I
later discovered is a holy mountain for the Nepalese people
and no-one is allowed to climb it. It is on the border of Tibet in a special area known as the Annapurna Sanctuary. I
had been befriended by one of the lovely Sherpa guides on
that first trek, and was able to arrange to return ten months
later in October 1989 for a private trek into the Sanctuary. Looking back, it was quite miraculous how this was
arranged and everything fell into place for me to make this
pilgrimage, for this is what the journey had become.

'From the moment I first saw Machapuchare I was
aware of an 'etheric Star' shining above its beautiful trian-
gular peak, and I knew inwardly that here was a meeting
place for illumined brethren working at the inner level to
help humanity on earth – brethren I had come to know
through my lifelong work with White Eagle and the Star
Brotherhood. My first trip had been "an adventure travel
holiday"; this second visit had a deep spiritual purpose. I
just "knew" I had to go. The Star was calling me!

'And so I set off for my trek with my Sherpa friend, Dil,

to help me, and staying at mountain "lodges" on the way. As we came nearer and nearer to the Sanctuary, it was as though the holy aura of the mountain reached out to enfold and uplift me. I am not naturally a mountain walker, and so physically the journey was very hard indeed for me. I was exhausted when we finally climbed up and over the last pass and entered the Sanctuary. Then came a big test for me – we could see nothing at all! A heavy mist had descended. I crawled into my tent despondent, and slept.

'I awoke suddenly some hours later and looked out of my tent. I shall never forget the vista which met my eyes! A clear starlit sky and mountains in a full circle all around me – for this is what the Sanctuary comprises, a high plateau surrounded on all sides by some of the greatest Himalayan peaks. I knew then indeed that at the etheric level it IS a meeting place for the Star Brotherhood. Wrapped in my sleeping bag, in the bitter cold of a mountain dawn, I watched the sun rise up behind Machapuchare. In the photograph I took – see front cover – it appears almost as a Star! My Master – the illumined being I have come to know as "The Master of the Star", who is the Master on the John ray and who is bringing the new age of Aquarius into being at this present time – came to me at this sunrise hour. This great one spoke with me and prepared me inwardly for the work which was to lie ahead.

'In October 2000, eleven years later, I was able to return a second time to the Sanctuary, accompanied at the inner level by my beloved ex-husband Geoffrey, to place in the Sanctuary one of our seven specially-programmed Earth Healing crystals. Again, my Master came to me to bless me, and encourage me in my work.'

A Personal Search: the Andes

'Just under a year later, in August 2001, I set out on another pilgrimage – this one to follow the old Inca trail across the Andes to the lost city of Machu Picchu. (I have often thought how interesting it is that this name is so similar to my special Himalayan mountain!). I found this trek particularly hard as the Inca trail has huge stone steps inserted going up, up, up, then down, down, down … on and on and on. I was almost literally on my knees in utter exhaustion. The night before what we were told was the hardest part (over a place aptly named "Dead Woman's Pass"!) I prayed more than ever for help and heard White Eagle saying very clearly, "We will give you wings of light". He did! I almost literally "flew up the mountainside" with an enormous burst of energy. That evening, elated at this "miracle", I knew it was the right moment to bury the earth healing crystal I had brought for the Andes. It was not to be in the Machu Picchu itself (too many people visiting), but in a remote place away from the trail.

'After five hard days I reached the ruins of the "City of Gold", which many tourists now visit. Most come now by mountain train from the beautiful city of Cuzco to marvel at the location and the magical, mysterious atmosphere of this place. If you are able to visit in the early morning (as I did) when no one is there, or the late afternoon when the last train has left, you may find that a peace has descended upon the place that fills the heart with warmth. It is easy here to tune in to the great mountain devas and the ceremonies and rituals of past civilizations. It was here, in the peace and magic of the next day's dawn, that again my "Master" came to talk with me.

'Even if you cannot come to this extraordinary place in your physical body, come in thought there now with me … by means of visualization and in your "body of light". Fly like the eagles and condors, soar above the mountain peaks in the clear air – free of earthly thought! Feel the great sense of freedom from earthly limitation and wonder at the majesty of God's creation and human endeavour. Find a high place to rest above the ancient ruins and wait…. What experience will unfold for you? Certainly a great blessing.

A Personal Search: Tibet
'As a traveller in search of spiritual inspiration you have to be prepared for sometimes very mixed vibrations and often harsh and materialistic influences. However, the in-

ner spiritual heart of Tibet can be felt strongly and clearly in the wide, open spaces of the vast plateaux and glorious mountains.

'A different experience from visiting the mountains, but an incredibly moving and deep one, is to go to Tibet's capital city, Lhasa, and mingle with the hundreds of pilgrims there. I felt Tibet's spiritual heart beating so strongly in Lhasa's famous Barkhor Square and Jokhang Temple. This temple is the most revered religious building in the whole of Tibet. Even before nearing its entrance the senses are touched on every level. The heavy fragrance of the huge sage-burning incense vats which are placed at many strategic points around the temple area, in Barkhor Square and around the "Pilgrim Circuit", fill the air. Also filling the air are the numerous other "fragrances" including the yak-butter lamps which burn within the main temple and in nearby surrounding chapels.

'The sounds are numerous too, but perhaps most evocative of all is the chanting of the monks, the proffered prayers and the oft-repeated "AUM MANI PADME HUM" of the many pilgrims as they turn the prayer wheels which line the temple entrance. There are also prayer wheels on both sides of the splendid Jokhang temple. At the temple entrance another remarkable sight greets the visitor. Here there are large numbers of worshippers prostrating themselves on the ground, going through an exercise and prayer routine similar to the "Salutation to the Sun" of yoga.

'I found the whole experience of the temple approach deeply moving and the feeling continued as I walked into the temple itself with its many flickering lamps. Twice during my days in Lhasa I walked seven times around the outer pilgrim circuit. This leads clockwise around the outside of the temple and Barkhor Square. During these circuits I felt that I was lifted in consciousness to a higher plane (not hard at this high altitude) and was aware of the inner heart of Tibet and the shining Star radiating a spiritual essence of peace and healing to the whole material world.'

Dragon Hill, Berkshire, England

The book, THE LIGHT IN BRITAIN, tells of the pilgrimage to the sacred places in Britain that was undertaken by Grace and Ivan Cooke, with Jenny Dent accompanying them. This extract, which begins with the words of Ivan Cooke, describes the spiritual experience they had on Dragon Hill, a site under the Berkshire Downs:

'What of that sweeter, brighter age of long before, of those more brotherly times when it is said men lived for perhaps double our present lifespan, wise and intelligent, and close to their beneficent God?

'To find out these things we have become pilgrims, like many others.... We have come to a place where mighty happenings have been wrought, and soon we are going to employ the power of clear vision, of clear seeing, that aspect of clear seeing which is the power to investigate ancient truths of long ago, to re-establish them in the thought and mind, and possibly in the very being of man; so that he sees whence he came and, better, knows why he is here, and gets more than a glimpse, a hope – gets a firm

belief as to whither he will go when his days in the flesh
are ended. In short, this is a clear seeing which can reveal
to a human being a world that although it seems disorder-
ly is in fact ordered and planned, with destiny clear before
the individual, and the reason for being and the way he or
she should try to live.

'Here we must explain that all physical form has its
etheric counterpart, and that all human life and thought
impresses itself on the 'ether' or the etheric emanation
from the physical life of our earth. The life a person leads
leaves an impression on the ether around them. Even the
commonplace, the ordinary life, leaves such an impression
– if any life is ever ordinary. But where some wise and
kind being has lived and worked, the impression remains
for ever. Thus the lives of all the ancient peoples who once
walked the earth are indelibly impressed upon the ether.
The few thousand years ago we cite are but a tale of yes-
terday....

'During the damp and chilly July of 1966 we three –
my wife, Jenny and myself – visited Dragon Hill, this time
travelling from Charney in Berkshire where we were staying for a few days. Despite the weather, Dragon Hill had
in no way lost its magical power, as will be apparent from
the scope and deeply mystical quality of the message received on this occasion, and which now follows.

'"I can see a vast gathering, but not of people of this
earth. They are visitors from the etheric world. I can see
these people perambulating the hillside, but what I am
seeing all took place very long ago. Great angels surround
us, the angels of the elements. Angels from the sun are
descending from the heavens. I see a most wonderful

light descending on Dragon Hill. Dragon Hill itself looks like a vast grail cup from which a beautiful gentle light is now rising. From these heights I can see the sun blazing, and framed in its light is the Christ figure, with arms outstretched pouring light like a blessing of love into the 'grail cup'. This 'cup' represents the real heart of Britain. The watching and worshipping concourse reaches out and up towards the light. Indeed I see humanity as a whole race yearning for this spiritual illumination, and in response, the Christ figure (the Christ, not Jesus) is reaching down, concentrating love and light on the earth. Again I see the brethren perambulating the hill, and at certain periods they turn inwards and raise their arms towards the light and towards this great symbolic figure.

"'The dragon is a symbol of the struggle between the forces of light and darkness. "'Then this great Christ figure comes. The people are revived and strengthened by the light. All this represents a tremendous spiritual effort. There is fierce combat between the light and the dark forces. After a long battle the dragon is gradually overcome and slain. At last it lies dead.

"'Then I see again what I have described before – the hill flooded with light. The vast 'grail cup' is there again and the white essence it contains is poured out over the land.

"'Something here feels most gentle, comforting and warm…. I can feel warmth all round me. I would say this was a particularly powerful centre of the grail ritual which goes far, far back, far beyond the Christian era to the very ancient brotherhood, and has been enacted again and again on the inner planes. Most beautiful rituals, beautiful ceremonies, were enacted by these people in bygone days.

These rituals will come back into use again, and become a great feature of the life of man. When man understands, when he learns how to commune with etheric and angelic forces – as he will – he will discover that he has within himself the potentialities of God his Creator. He will learn how to create ideal form from the white ether. He will have power, knowledge and wisdom enough to use not only stone and brick, but the white ether itself with which to build his temples for the worship of his Creator.

'"Something uniquely pure and holy is here. It is this very purity and simplicity which is the saving grace of humanity. Humanity must learn the meaning of the light and how to use the spiritual sunlight from the Solar Logos, the purity and holiness of which is man's salvation. This is the reason for the work and ritual of our Brotherhood of the White Eagle Lodge – to project the rays of the pure light out to all people, as the brotherhoods have done from ancient times. Here is the point of balance of positive and negative forces between construction and destruction, which meet here. The forces of light will always triumph."'

The English Downland

The power of the hilltops is described by Geoffrey Hayward in his article 'The Holy Hills', from the White Eagle magazine *Stella Polaris*.

'All over the southern downland of England are hilltop fortresses called variously Castles, Camps or Rings, from the great earthwork banks and ditches encircling them as defences. But these heavy defences are often the work of later peoples, such as the Celts who occupied the strongholds at the time of the Roman Invasion of Britain; for indeed many of these hilltops were the sites of ancient sun-temples belonging to earlier and more peaceful races.

'From these heights there can be seen far and wide over the bare downland, with its hills rising and falling into the distance; sometimes through a distant valley is the blue of the sea; and over all, the vast, extending sky, depth within depth, in which is the sun like a fountain of light opened in the heaven. There is only the movement of the wind – or the call of a passing bird – to break the silence. Thus are clearly present to us, in this solitude of unbroken space, the four kingdoms of earth, water, air and fire: the wide earth, the distant far-stretching sea, the vast air and sky, and the mighty fire of the sun – or by night the great wheel of stars....

'The hill-tops of the downland were ... used as altars for the worship of The Great Light. Now an altar in a church symbolizes man's own inmost heart – the sanctuary, the holy of holies, where God is present. The people trod the paths up these hills, singing and praising God in all His ways; then they gathered in silence and great reverence, while the priests chanted; and that done, utter silence reigned. The people became truly aware of this Divine Presence; they felt the fire of His love descend upon them, and in their own hearts the responsive fire. The fire came down to them, the fire ascended from their hearts.

There was thus a jointure, a marriage of heaven and earth. The fire radiated from their hearts, it made nature quick beside them. The holy fire passed into the earth, causing it to quicken and radiate the white fire of life.

'These hills thus became great centres of power. For earth, too, like man has embedded on it the white fire. Many have noticed the subtle atmosphere of these sacred places, one more of light than of heaviness – a more ethereal atmosphere which can be contacted by any percipient person. The atmosphere seems full of joy, the air like blithe wine, and there is a sense of music around; one feels very near the presence of ancient brethren, and close to the Sun. These are but the results of the ancient Sun Worship – of the Spiritual Sun.'

A Mountain in Southern France

Colum Hayward shares a personal experience of a long trek he made that brought him closer to the heart of the Cathar 'secret'. He begins by referring back to the extract on pp. 65–8.

'Separating Minesta's special château of Lordat from the more famous Cathar stronghold at Montségur there rises a mountain of some 7500 feet, very roughly 2500 metres. Three-quarters of the height of the Pyrenean ridge behind it to the south, it stands more or less solo and holds majesty over the most famous area associated with the Cathars. Its western slopes drop steeply, with Lordat perched on the edge of the gorge carved out by the Ariège. To the east, it tapers more gently, and thus drops to the land of the Aude, the other great river of the Languedoc.

'The thought once held me that if there was an escape from Montségur, the obvious way of concealment

was over the mountain, and it felt to me most suggestive
that the small château of Lordat should be directly over
the mountain. That might fit beautifully with the apparent search for buried treasure by members of the Polaires
in Minesta's day. So one August or September, quite a few
years ago, finding myself retreating from the Pyrenees
because of a stomach bug, I realized I had an ideal opportunity to make the journey on foot that maybe Cathar
knights had taken seven hundred years before.

'Later research I've done scarcely backs up my view, but
the pilgrimage was eventful. First, I arrived in Montségur
weak from my virus, still quite unable to eat. How could
I contemplate a high mountain walk over two days and
nights, carrying a tent, in that condition? My body itself
gave the answer. I had a sudden intimation that I needed
the juice of the quince fruit, and that that would settle my
stomach.

'Montségur is a tiny village and I've never even located
the shop on subsequent visits. Yet on that occasion I found
myself in a general store without even searching. Inside,
among everything from ironmongery to fresh vegetables,
was the largest selection of fruit juices I've ever seen. I
didn't even know the French for 'quince' but the picture
on the label was enough. I bought two 1.5-litre bottles.

'They literally kept me going to the top of the mountain. On and on, resting frequently, I nonetheless felt sufficiently the better for the quince juice to keep going. It
would last me to the top. I felt it had been sent to me.

'I spent one night not very far up, and woke to the
awareness that my tent was quite surrounded by timber
trucks. So well had I slept I'd never heard them. I'm not

sure if I, or the lumbermen, were more surprised when
I put my head out of the tent flap. My second night was
beside the summit. I remember the chill, the excitement
of having got there, and the joy of settling the tent down
into some soft undergrowth to give a springy bed. A wild,
remote landscape in no way related to valley life.

'Then I remember the steep descent and how long it
seemed to take – descents always surprise in that way –
and the little reascent to the château at Lordat. Dramatic,
its rock looks to be – from this side just as much as from
the deep gorge beyond it. But did I count out the footsteps
of Cathar knights? I don't remember doing so.

'And yet the mountain holds my imagination still. Today it is generally known as the Pic de St-Barthélèmy
(Peak of St Bartholomew), but its other name is the Montagne de Tabe. That 'Tabe' is generally reckoned to be
borrowed from the name Mount Tabor, the mountain in
the Holy Land associated with the Transfiguration of Jesus. Certain writers have been fascinated by this, and seen
it as a hill full of symbolic power, transforming the character of the area from a beautiful landscape into a holy
place. Somehow, I am inclined to agree. When the sun
strikes the face of the mountain from the west, it really
does seem to be a hill of light. When – as it often is – it is
covered with snow, it is still, indeed even more, a mountain of light.

'One of the things that today holds my imagination
about the Cathars is that through their rituals and through
the very strength of their beliefs they made death insignif-
icant. They held a secret we long for in our century, that
of walking from one state of life into another with indif-

ference as to the change of state. The light was so real for them in the consciousness they had awakened on earth, that death held no surprises – even when it was violent death. Even to enter the flames was a moment only of walking into the light.

'And what is the story of the Transfiguration? It comes in the gospels of Matthew, Mark and Luke, and it is the moment when high on a mountain Jesus begins to shine with light. The dictionary tells us that transfiguration describes "a complete change of form or appearance into a more beautiful or spiritual state". Jesus is greeted from the invisible as "My Son", and the disciples with him are asked not to speak of an event that seems to prefigure the Ascension. "Tell the vision to no man, until the Son of man be risen again from the dead." Jesus has demonstrated the power he holds to walk between two worlds, and this mountain of the Transfiguration, Tabor in the Languedoc, reveals its mystery in the light I see upon it when I look. There is no death.'

The Stone Monuments of Britain

Although we often see a spiritual pilgrimage as a personal thing, sometimes a group endeavour can help to make the experience more meaningful. Here Jeremy Hayward describes how the insight of others can help to bring inspiration. The monument of which he speaks dates back over five thousand years.

'Some years ago quite a large party of Lodge members undertook a four-day walk from Avebury stone circle back to New Lands, where the White Eagle Temple in England stands. This hike was in aid of the Temples in Australia and America, still both about to be. I remember we started the walk in thick mist, assembling together by the stones briefly to send out the light as a group. There were just a few damp and curious cows for company. Our path skirted around Silbury Hill, following the willow-lined steam which will be familiar to many visitors to the area, and then crossed the trunk road to yet another of the many megalithic monuments in this wonderful area of southern England – the West Kennet Long Barrow. We stopped just a few minutes there, exploring both the small, damp chambers inside the barrow, and standing for a while on the long ridge of its back. We had a day's walk and twenty miles before us and needed to move on.

'I remember, however, talking to a fellow walker later, a dear brother of the Lodge from Florence, and when I asked her if she had been able to feel any special atmosphere at the long barrow, her words rang very true to me. "It was almost", she said, "That you could feel there was no difference there between life and death". To readers who have never been to West Kennet, nor to many others of these ancient barrows in Britain, her words may sound cryptic, but she expressed for me something I had tried to put into words on many previous visits to the barrow, when I had been exploring the whole, inspiring Avebury area.

'Though of enormous interest archaeologically, the West Kennet Long Barrow is not immediately prepossessing to a purely casual visitor. There are the imposing stones at the entrance, but the primitive burial chambers inside, which one can explore with a bent head and back, are naturally rather dank, often muddy underfoot, and not without a sprinkling of twentieth-century litter. On top one can walk along the fifty-yard-long ridge, admiring the views of the Marlborough and Pewsey Downs all around, which seem to make a bowl in the landscape, a bowl of which Avebury is the centre.

'The stones making the walls and roof of the chambers are not of course in any way shaped, and there is no doubting the technological simplicity of the barrow's builders. What it is difficult to doubt, either, however, is the potency of atmosphere one can touch upon – something of far more substance than just the romantic feeling of standing by a construction of such enormous antiquity. The atmosphere of the burial chambers I can only describe as a deep stillness – yet a stillness very different from, say, the hush and awe of a Christian cathedral. There is a feeling of the stilling of all life's passion and a power wholly benevolent but almost, as our brother said, indifferent to life and death. I have no doubt that these places were associated with ceremonies of the passage from the physical life, and there is another strange feature that I am sure many visitors have experienced in the same way I have. This is that lying or standing on top of the barrow, there is, almost in contrast to the stillness, a feeling of wonderful light and sweetness.

'It is probably my fancy that wild flowers bloom here

and in similar places in a special profusion (and even if true, one practical reason for this is that such areas are fenced off from grazing). But I remember especially one hot July day lying in the long grass and taking photographs of the flowers as they were caught by the setting summer sun, and feeling beneath this outward sweetness a most wonderful purity, lightness and freedom.

'One summer I spent a week in a very different part of Britain – the Orkney Isles. Apart from the beauty of the northern islands and their wildlife, we had gone there to give ourselves the opportunity of visiting the remarkable number of ancient sites on Orkney – especially the stones of the Ring of Brodgar. This is one of the most stunningly situated stone circles in Britain, and believed to be contemporary with Callanish on the Isle of Lewis.

'For me personally, however, the site on Orkney which left the deepest and most inspiring impression was a far more humble one. Towards the end of our stay we visited Unstan's chambered tomb. This is a burial mound lying on a little promontory across the water from Brodgar. It is outwardly not at all the most impressive of burial sites left by megalithic peoples on Orkney, although it is very early, being at least four thousand years old. The mound has been partly reconstructed after excavation.

'One enters through a little passage four feet high into the central chamber, which is divided into individual compartments by upright slabs of stone which protrude from the side walls. There is so little inside which is physically remarkable to eyes such as my own, which are untrained in archaeology. One huddles between the damp stone walls and ponders on what it is which evokes a sense of reverence far more than just the interest in something of such antiquity. I found myself remembering as I sat there those words, "you could feel that there was no difference there between life and death". The feeling here too, although subtle as all such impressions necessarily are, was of a deep stillness; not just a hushed or numinous atmosphere but, in a way not dissimilar from West Kennet, a feeling of the complete stillness of all earthly passions.

It was a different quality from anything I had ever felt in a building of Christian era, a power totally benign, but so still as to feel quite impersonal. Indeed it was beyond all personality. I stayed there for some minutes and then came out along the little passage way into the sunlight. Almost unconsciously I felt I should be offering thanks at what was truly such a holy place, biut in a strange way, my thanks seemed just irrelevant before a power so still, so ancient and impersonal.

'I sat on top of the mound and looked down at the shorelines a few yards away, and over the Loch of Stenness, peaceful in the evening sun. Right down to the seaweed's edge were meadowsweet, pink campion and wild grasses; and across the other side, cows, just standing at the water's edge. Behind, on the skyline, were the humped-backed hills of Hoy, which the mound of the barrow almost seems to echo in its shape. It was a scene in which any visitor would find sweetness, and yet here too the natural beauty seemed to echo an inner fragrance. It was as if on top of the barrow everything was light. The air for me held the magic of a joy beyond all mortality.

'I felt I could have stayed there unhurried and happy through the long northern evening. Even though we did leave I felt I still lived for the rest of the day in the atmosphere I had been privileged to touch.

'Of course there have been many occasions when I have visited similar sites and really been aware of nothing in particular at all, or only a glimmer. Maybe not all these ancient barrows were places of such power, or maybe in some places that power has receded beyond our ability now to normally touch it; and of course, too, I am sure that making such a contact is in a way a special gift to us and depends on conditions in ourselves being right to receive it. It is also true, I think, that the energy and atmosphere of these sites is by no means identical. For instance, clearly visible across the water from Unstan's chambered tomb, about a mile and a half away, lies the far more famous chamber of Maes Howe. This is dated archaeologically about five hundred years later than Unstan and architecturally is undoubtedly the most remarkable chambered tomb in Britain. The roof and walls of the passage into the central chamber are formed by monumental slabs of stone, over five metres in length, and the rays of the midwinter sunrise penetrate down this narrow passage to fall on the dry stone masonry of the chamber itself. I have never been to Egypt, but making our way down the passage to the central chamber felt as I have always imagined entry into one of the pyramids would feel. The whole feeling to us here was of great solar, almost regal, power, and certainly I have never known a mound of earth seem to command the surrounding landscape with such magisterial presence.

'I am sure, as I have said, that these sites were associated with ceremonies to do with the passage from physical life;

but also, in a way of which we have lost understanding, of entry into everlasting life. Perhaps it is not important for us to know now what these ceremonies were, and certainly there seems likely never to be archaeological evidence to help us understand the spiritual power to which these outwardly simple, even primitive, peoples, must have lived so close. But alongside the more arresting stone circles that we usually think of as signs of "the Light of Britain", surely also these quiet mounds live as mounds of peace for us, places where once souls knew the consciousness of eternal life.'

Wild Nature in Australia

Pilgrimage can be inspired by places of ritual and ceremony, such as a cathedral, but also by sites of wild and natural beauty. In her pilgrimages, Lyn Edwards, Mother of the White Eagle Lodge in Australasia, shares her experience of pilgrimage in that continent. Uluru is the place once known as Ayers Rock.

Wild Nature: Antarctica & The Apostles
'The continent of Australia falls sharply away into the Southern Ocean with twelve columns of harder rock standing valiantly and steadfastly as the waves buffet them. They are known as the Twelve Apostles – a fitting name for it links them with those twelve brave and advanced souls who came to the earth to assist the Master Jesus in his mission. Those disciples withstood the winds of the mind whipping up turbulent seas of emotion after the Master's passing.

'Standing on the high cliffs overlooking these twelve columns, you find the wind is always strong and biting, carrying the vibration of the pure Southern Ocean. There is no other land between you and Antarctica and the powerful force of this southern continent is overwhelming.

'Each continent has its master and its wise ones who have the land in their care. There are also the angels of the land. One would tend to think of Antarctica as sleeping, covered in snow, as if the life-force has been withdrawn, waiting for a birth....

'However, standing on the cliffs looking towards Antarctica one becomes aware of the Great Mother holding vibrant life within her folds. Antarctica is teeming with life and the Southern Ocean is alive with myriad forms of life from the tiny krill to the great whales. The force of the continent holds powerful, raw energy like none other I have ever experienced. I have stood on the shores of the Indian, Pacific and Atlantic Oceans but none have the power and majesty and the quality of life-force of the Southern Ocean. There are only two words with which to describe this conjunction of land and ocean – raw power. It is the power of Creation, the power of the Great Mother.

'So will you stand with me now on the cliffs of the Great Ocean Road in southern Victoria, face turned towards Antarctica, arms outstretched with the strong wind buffeting our face, hair, body? It is exhilarating. The magical raw creative energy flows up from Antarctica. The Apostle rocks stand as sentinels, filtering this energy like the twelve constellations filter the universal energy. You may wish to choose one particular rock and absorb its energy, as though meditating on your astrological sign, or you may wish to work with an element or mode. Whatever you chose, be aware of this filtered energy coming to you from the Great Mother energy of Antarctica.

As a Scorpio, I feel the great angels of that sign like a great rush of wind energy lifting me, higher, higher, as on eagle's wings, above the mire of everyday life and problems into my heavenly body of light where I can overcome all difficulties, all testing. Just let this Great Mother energy lift you, too, into your heavenly body of light – where all is well. Here, at this level of consciousness, we can adjust the molecules of our physical body, using this raw creative energy to bless the very cells of our being.'

Wild Nature: the Great Barrier Reef
'Although it is made up of numerous individual reefs, coral cays and islands, the Great Barrier Reef is one identity stretching from the north-eastern tip of Australia to Bundaberg in central Queensland. Each individual component has its own angel and spirit, I believe, and all these are under the direction of the great angel of the reef who holds the teeming life both on the land and in the waters within his or her being. This great angel is golden in colour and yet. like the mother-of-pearl shell which holds a blend of all the pastel colours, the vibrant colours of the reef are also reflected within the body of the golden angel – the vivid blues and greens of the waters, the pure white of the sands, the multicoloured corals and fish. Seen from the air, the reef is stunning. Seen from beneath the waters, the reef is alive, living, pulsating, and this same feeling of pulsating life is held within its great angel.

'We mostly think of the masters as being in the Himalayas or the Andes, yet I believe that somewhere high above the throng yet on one of the headlands in far northern Queensland there is a home of one of the Masters, not quite in the physical but close. Visiting this beautiful Master in his special place one can stand at the end of the grassy headland, just a few feet above the waterline, looking out on the mostly calm blue sea – the Coral Sea. This is part of the Pacific Ocean – and Pacific itself means peaceful. All oceans can be tumultuous and storm-tossed at times, yet the feeling of the Pacific is generally one of peace.

'The gentle sea breeze carrying this peace cools the air and we look back to the open building set in the gardens. Allemande, hibiscus, bougainvillea add a riot of colour to the scene. Here, in the midst of all this beauty, is someone so gentle yet so strong. He comes forward, as if appearing from nowhere. Eyes of pure love look deeply into yours. We are transfixed by his eyes and the purity of his love. The vibrant colours of our surroundings fade into nothingness as we are caught up in the feeling of love. Bathe in this vibration; let it fill every cell of your being on every level of your being. As your being is filled with love, become aware of the peace carried to you in waves from the ocean, washing over you. We quietly sit within the aura of the Master and absorb his wisdom. What is he teaching you?

'As he gently leaves, we become aware again of the frangipani, its colour, its perfume. The colourful parrots feast in the trees. The breeze is ruffling our hair. The smell of the ocean is fresh and clean. We are at peace. Love fills our hearts. This sojourn with the Master has been special and we are blest.'

Wild Nature: Uluru

'As we leave the fertile green rim of Australia, especially on the eastern coast, and venture towards the heart of the country, pulled by that indescribable calling to "the Heart", we drive hour after hour, day after day through flat, seemingly lifeless, desolate country. In those long lonely miles something happens to our inner being and the dull landscape transforms as our eyes are opened to the subtle beauty. Is this not the same as our journey through life? What appears boringly mundane is actually filled with higher beauty, if only we have the eyes to see.

'The expanse of the cobalt blue sky is immense and shouts "freedom!". It is a freedom that comes from an atmosphere clear of human thought-forms, as most of the Outback has not been walked upon and the population is so sparse. This inner freedom from other people's thoughts or even centuries of thoughts is like eagle wings lifting the soul right into the heart of the Sun.

'The air might be dusty but its inner essence is clean: clean of pollutants, clean of thought-pollution. It carries the dust, the essence of the earth, the beautiful, red earth, as if the blood from the heart has carried its essence into the very soil.

'Through the desert, the tracks lead us closer. We can

feel the pulse of the heart, calling, calling us to the centre of this great land which is held within the care of the wise and ancient ones: the soul of Australia. The colours of the land – the brilliant ochre, the lavenders, purples, soft pinks – all heal, bathe and renew our senses and prepare us as we come closer and closer to the heart of this land.

'And so, on our approach, the scenery becomes magnificent. As we come over a rise we can see in the distance 'the heart' indeed. We stop in awe, breathing in the heartbeat of the land, bathed in its radiance. As we come closer we realize how huge the rock is – 3.6 kms (nearly 2.5 miles) long, 1.9 kms (1.2 miles) wide, and with a circumference of 9.4 kms (nearly 6 miles). As you stand at the base you look up the 348 meters (1141 ft) of this massive monolith, knowing that 2.5 kms (1.5 miles) of its bulk is underground.

'Standing quietly, your whole being resonates to this grand heartbeat, and it makes you want to fall on your knees in gratitude and in awe of the power that is emanating from this heart chakra of Australia. Some also call it the Solar Plexus centre of the world. The angel of Uluru is immense, both in size and in power, yet utterly peaceful. Vibrant red, the colour of the earth, tinged with gold, his–her radiance covers the whole of Australia.

'As the sun begins to set, we make our way towards the campsite some few kilometres from Uluru but still within the powerful vibration of this chakra, thankful to the Pitjantjatjara people for their loving care of this sacred site. We turn and pause, watching Uluru's light change to a kaleidoscope of breathtaking colour as the sun quickly drops beneath the western horizon. The fading rays of the sun seem to ignite the inner light of the rock like an inner flame and the intense blessing of the site and the angel burst forth in clarion shouts of life and joy. As it does, our inner flame responds and leaps with joy and wonder into ever expanding life.

'Our pilgrimage to the heart, to the centre, to Uluru is as much about the journey as it is about this sacred site, the destination. Both are important.'

The Labyrinth

Pilgrimage does not always mean travelling a long distance...the journey can be a symbolic one. Previously, Jenny Dent wrote about the spiritual significance of a labyrinth. Walking a labyrinth is in itself a pilgrimage. The chapter continues with shorter accounts in which different people describe their experiences.

The Labyrinth: Chartres Cathedral
'I had written a little prayer I could recite as I walked the labyrinth. But as I began to walk I thought I might be wrong and should say the Lord's Prayer instead. As I started I realized it was right to say my prayer:

'I love you, Dear God, and hold you in my heart;
'I love you, Dear God, for all the love you give;
'I love you, Dear God, in all Thou art;
'I love you, Dear God, with all my heart.

'I ended at the centre with ... I hold you in my heart, which surprised me but in the same instant I heard quite clearly: "As you are held in mine".

'I somehow staggered to a pew to try and absorb the enormity of this. It was a wondrous moment I shall always treasure.'

L.H.

The Labyrinth: White Eagle Land, Montgomery, Texas
'I clear my mind of all thoughts of the outer world, remove my shoes and begin slow and steady steps on the red bricks.

'At first I find myself looking down at the tiny tufts of weed and minute yellow flowers that are beginning to push between the bricks towards the sunlight. Then, consciously, I lift my eyes to the distant trees and become aware of the twittering and cheeping of the birds. How is it that I had not heard them before this? It feels as though I am climbing a gentle slope, a narrow pathway around a hill. The colours of the trees seem brighter – vibrant greens and browns, the blossom seems alive. This is a true meditation. The circles are becoming smaller. I seem to have companions, yet there is no-one else here today. It is almost as if there are three or four or five of us steadily climbing this path. The sunlight streams through the branches of a tall tree, feeding its warmth into my mind. Suddenly, like Tenzing Norgay first summitting Everest, I am at the top. The path is finished. I close my eyes and stand, arms outstretched, to embrace the sunlight, the birds, the trees, the joy of life, heaven.'

S.N.

The Labyrinth: Lightning Ridge, Australia
'The track led off the main road into the black opal mining town of Lightning Ridge. A little further on from this

miner's haven was a large labyrinth laid out with stone of white, soft pink and red. Like all labyrinths the journey takes you on a woven path in to the centre and back out again. As I wandered this journey, it spoke of our many lifetimes, first going one way, then the next.

'Walking carefully through this maze, shifting stones back into place where needed, I suddenly realized my whole focus was on the ground. On this journey I needed to look up and out and see the magnificent scenery. Isn't this so often the way with our lives, too? We are so caught up with our happenings that we forget to look at the beauty which surrounds us. So I walked carefully, stopping frequently to look around me.

'The labyrinth was a large one which seemed to take a long time to complete. When finally I emerged, I felt what must be akin to the feeling of utter freedom and joy we must feel when we have completed our journey and have no further need to reincarnate.'

L.E.

Some Individual Tales of Pilgrimage

Pilgrimage is an intensely personal thing. We all experience it in different ways and view places with different eyes. Over the next few pages several people on the White Eagle spiritual path share their experiences of pilgrimage at sites around the world.

Ephesus, Turkey

'I visited Kasadusi in Turkey and went on a tour for the ruins of Ephesus. This is where I had a profound spiritual experience. On the tour, the guide told us about the House of the Virgin Mary. This house was rediscovered around the late 1800s, solely through the visions of a German nun. In 1891 an expedition set out to find the house described in the visions. Eventually the ruins of the house were found by three priests. Since then the area has been proclaimed a Holy Site, and more than a million people visit per year. Three popes have visited the house and have said Mass there. It is a holy shrine visited by both Christians and Muslims.

'At the front of the house before entering is a sign asking for complete silence and no photography. I slowly walked under the stone arch and immediately I felt a sensation of peace upon my body. There was a chair to the side of the small room which I sat on.

'As soon as I sat down I felt goosebumps from my head to my feet. Tears welled up in my eyes and I started to cry. My heart felt as though it was expanding and opening to an amazing energy, which I felt was out of this world. The sensation lasted about a minute and it was the highlight of my trip. It was unexpected and I knew without a doubt that I had made a connection with Divine Mother. I feel certainly that it was also a soul memory of being there in a previous incarnation. Since that experience I have felt even more connections and the love of Divine Mother. The earth holds within it beautiful sacred energies imprinted throughout the ages: how blest I am to have felt them.'

L.H.

Avebury

'Coming down from the long hill,
The circles print their powerful image on our eyes,
Each arching stone blending with the next,
Giving and receiving and returning – one life –
One all-embracing love.
Closer,
    and we lose ourselves in the magic
And the nearness of the Light,
Slowing,
    until we move in rhythmic, ritual dance amongst
    the stones.
Grey sentinels holding the form of our creative spell,
We step between you and are hushed
By time and timeless; by the immutable
And all that is different.
The earth shifts, and is still under our willing feet;
We tread lovingly
As high notes rise in a waking sky; deep chords echo
    in earth;
The stones between receiving: air and earth, rain
    and mystic fire –
Our boundaries dissolving with sound....
'We are standing in the silence at the centre

Where the rose makes manifest.
The dawn's light sliding over the dewed rim
And flowing delicately to the heart –
This gentle earth again baptised,
The stones saluting the Sun.'

A.H.

The Pipes of Old: an Avebury Moment

'I and a small group of friends had decided to go up to Avebury, to the four-and-a-half-thousand-year-old ceremonial stone circles, to experience the gathering that occurred there for the Autumn Equinox. The Equinox is the moment when night and day are exactly the same length, twelve hours, and that year it occurred on Sunday 22nd September.

'We got up to Avebury late on the Friday. The sun had already set, so after setting up our tents, with great difficulty in the dark, we set off to the central meeting place: the seventeenth-century thatched pub called The Red Lion. Many people had travelled to Avebury for the Equinox, people from all over the country; Scotland, Wales, London and across the south; even as far afield as the Czech Republic and Australia. There was such a strong feeling of communion there; everyone I met was so open and welcoming that from the very first moment I felt at ease.

'The gathering of people was vibrant, full of beautiful souls, colourful characters and inspiring musicians. I had found myself in the middle of a group of musicians from Aberdeen. There was Alan who played the flute, Rog with his collection of singing bowls and Alistair who played an African drum called a djembe.

'Mindful of how late it was getting and not wishing to disturb the locals, the group of ten or twelve of us decided to take our celebrations into the stone circles. Now it is well documented that the stones on the inner circles are positioned in such a way that any sound made on the inside of them creates an echo and the sound waves ricochet and reverberate off the standing stones. Well aware of this, Alistair the djembe drummer took us all to a specific stone he liked to call the neolithic amplifier. Twelve to fourteen feet in height and about as wide, it was an imposing stone situated at the north of the southern inner circle.

'With his back to the stone and the mouth of his drum directed straight at it, Alistair started up a tribal rhythm that pulsed and reverberated across the enclosure. All of us started to feel it rising up through our feet and resonating within our chest. Then we found ourselves dancing and chanting, singing and laughing with joy, as the drum pounded and the Tibetan bowls sang out, lifting our hearts. The rhythm, singing, chanting and dancing reached a crescendo and with a final boom it came to a stop. Clapping and cheering we all congratulated each other for the part we had all played in that moment. Our group finally fell into a collective silence.

'Then from the west of the stones, emerging from the moonlit mists, came the sound of the bagpipes. These were the pipes of old, playing a tune that spoke of the ancient Celtic heartland. As he came striding towards us through the mist, the moonlight picked out the fiery redness of his hair, he came to a stop in front of us; his front leg cocked like a stag, pounding its hoof to the rhythm of the pipes. Then nonchalantly strolling up beside him, Alistair picked up the beat and the sound of the drums and the bagpipes spiralled around us, forcing us all to dance and jig and whoop with joy to this amazing music.

'I can't tell you how long they played for, but I prayed that it would never end. The enchantment of the music, like a faerie revelry, had taken hold of me and I would have been more than happy to dance into a faerie hill and disappear for all eternity. And then like consummate musicians, although these two had never played with each other before, at exactly the same time they came to a perfect stop.'

S.G.

Newgrange, in County Meath, Ireland

'One of the most remarkable megalithic sites in the world, Newgrange is a great mound faced with white quartz, aligned on the rising sun at the Winter Solstice when, for three mornings, the light enters the 'light box' above the entrance and travels right along the passage to illuminate the central chamber at the heart of the mound with a glorious golden light. It is an awe-inspiring enactment of the fertilizing sun entering the symbolic womb of Mother Earth.

'In meditation in the central chamber, along with several others, I was aware of an extraordinary vortex of energy spiralling up through the roof in the centre of the chamber.'

J.B.

Iona, Scotland

'It was meant to be a beautiful, deeply spiritual experience. The reality fell rather short of expectations. We were on the Isle of Iona, described by White Eagle as 'A lighthouse of the world. A centre of spiritual beauty'. Not described as 'freezing, really muddy, and with ancient remains hidden in the middle of nowhere'. We had started our trek in a balmy breeze which became bullet-like stinging rain; my eldest daughter was coughing in a manner suggesting she was about to die of consumption; we were ridiculously lost … and my son had just tripped over a hillock and fallen face down in a colossal puddle, with the result that he was literally mud-soaked from his eyebrows downwards. And we still hadn't found St Columba's hermitage.

'Just as I began to despair, unexpectedly, the skies cleared … and as a shaft of glorious sunlight speared down on to our shivering forms, I realized that the trials and tribulations were all part of the package. The path of a spiritual pilgrim was never meant to be an easy one. The journey of pilgrimage was like the journey of life, and it involved getting tired and muddy. And at that exact moment, we suddenly saw a circle of ancient stones that could only be the hermitage.

'It isn't possible to be in your own little spiritual bubble. Especially if you have children. But if you persist it can be worth it. I bribed for myself some moments alone in the hermitage and had the most beautiful meditation; even though it only lasted five minutes before I returned from glorious galloping white horses to the yells of 'Come on, Mummy'. Similarly, on the top of the hill, Dun-I,

I managed a short meditation gazing out over one of the most beautiful scenes I have ever witnessed – my inner eyes watching the blazing beacons of light springing out of the ancient rocks – before I was literally hit by a stone, thrown (accidentally, apparently) during an 'amusing' game. I was just getting started again when another group of people arrived unexpectedly at the summit. Ah well, I decided ruefully, glaring crossly at their day-glo anoraks obstructing my view. That's life!

'White Eagle tells us that we have to work for inner peace. We need to find our moments of peace and cultivate an inner stillness among the chaos. In today's world we cannot be shutting ourselves off from the rest of the world like ancient hermits, attractive though that vision sounds. Life as a spiritual pilgrim in the modern age is very different, but it can still be very rewarding. In fact, the spiritual pilgrimage, I realized later, can be seen as symbolic of the spiritual path through life.'

S.C.

The Little Temple for World Peace, Sri Lanka

This monument was created by the charity Star Action at the turn of the twenty-first century, and shows that sites do not have to be ancient to be places of pilgrimage.

'The sensation is that of being drawn by a strong magnet along a narrow, winding road between village houses, the scent of jasmine, oleander and temple flowers wafting on the warm evening air, until round the final corner I find the gateway to the Little Temple. Stepping stones in the sand between the palm trees lead me on and as I reach the circular building, its white pillars gleaming in the evening sun, I know I have come "home". Stepping inside onto the golden six-pointed star on the floor towards the circular central altar, touching its cool stone, I feel the presence of spirit and the links with guides and loved ones.

'Looking beyond this I gaze in wonder at the sea and the sparkling line of sunlight reaching across the glistening water seems like pathway to worlds unseen with an insistent impression that it links us with Africa. It is the hour of sunset and, as the sun inches its way down to the horizon, infusing the sky with shades of pink, purple and red, I sit in meditation with the feeling that I am not alone on this ancient site, but sharing the energy of the sun and the star with the whole of creation. It is so easy to meditate here, so much inspiration and so many deeply felt companions of the spirit. Since my first visit, for the dedication of the Little Temple, I have returned many times, ever more confident that this beautiful circular building on the beach, so simple and yet so perfect, is truly my little piece of paradise on earth, to which I may return in physical form or in meditation at home. The pilgrimage is not just physical but truly spiritual too, and is always there in my heart.'

E.V.

Tintagel, Cornwall

'A misty land where the boundaries between myth, legend and reality blur…. Tintagel is a deeply spiritual place for those who have eyes to see and ears to hear.: a place where the land undulates before your very eyes. It may be due to the shifting energies – many leylines meet and cross here. Cornwall's a land that presents many different faces.

'The pilgrim who visits this place must gain its respect; some are given the opportunity to experience spiritual lessons and the learning these offer. Balance and ground yourself when you arrive!

'Like many sacred places, Tintagel has its times of expansion and its times of stillness. It has times when many flock here and other times of stillness and quiet. A phrase that keeps springing to mind is 'hidden magic'. To find that magic, that light, the seeker must truly seek.

'There are many places where you may find peace and quiet away from the crowds. You may find one of the amazing white, quartz stones on the island to sit on and meditate while you are looking out to sea. Or you may walk in the footsteps of ancient Brothers to St Nectan's Glen, or Rocky Valley – but the one place where I find total peace is the little chapel dedicated to the Lady of Fontevrault, situated on the road that leads from the high street to the church on the cliff. I have often experienced deep peace and healing in this small, simple place of worship.'

S.W.

Rosslyn Chapel, Scotland

'In medieval times, before Rosslyn Chapel was built, Rosslyn was the last stage of the long pilgrimage from St James Cathedral in northern Spain, taking in Notre Dame and

Chartres Cathedrals. I am told that there were seven stages in all – each associated with one of the planets. Rosslyn was the final one and represented Saturn.

'The original pilgrimage was not Christian but Celtic and taken by Druids who revered the Earth Goddess. The medieval Christian church had suppressed this worship of the Mother spirit along with the order of the Knights Templar.

'Rosslyn Chapel is built on that place of spiritual power. Sacred music is the hidden mystery both in the architecture and in the mathematics of the musical scale. It could be said that there is, hidden in the sacred geometry of the architecture of the building, music in stone; and there are ornate carvings, as the chapel is encrusted with symbols in the stonework, some of Templar and Masonic origin.

'As a group we sat in the area called the Lady Chapel and, attuning ourselves to the light of the Star, we silently read our printed prayer for sending out the Light – and then one earthing the light in Scotland's grail cup, so the ancient spiritual flame may bring new awareness and healing for all. I became aware that Divine Mother was in my meditative thoughts as if she was guarding the sacred secrets, symbols and codes in the chapel, until the Mother Earth spirit from ancient times could rise again with safety (and not be suppressed as before) to give balance to the world and healing to Mother Earth. I think Rosslyn Chapel may be an expression of the sacred feminine in stone for those that have 'eyes to see and ears to hear'. Truth conquers all – if I dare say it!'

A.P.

Assisi, Italy

Assisi is a most popular place of pilgrimage, and was a favourite of Ylana Hayward, for many years Mother of the White Eagle Lodge. The following words, taken from the White Eagle magazine *Stella Polaris*, also indicate how well it pays to 'get away from the throng'.

'You know, I much prefer the word "Brother" to "Saint" because that is what Francis was, and is. He is truly one of the shining company, but what he demonstrated through his earthly life was a warm, real, humble realization of brotherhood – and of the power this brotherly spirit has to create beauty and goodness. It is a gift which still has an effect on life on earth today and on our personal lives. He is not far away.

'As many readers will know, I have had the opportunity to visit the Hermitage at Assisi more than once – and oh, the memories which come flooding in of moments of fulfilment and peace! I remember sitting with friends in the tiny cell used by our brother. I was troubled by the continual stream of talking visitors. For a moment, however, I was helped to feel the meaning of those words from his prayer – "Where there is injury, let me bring pardon". The words came, "Just love them".

'As my own attitude to the interruptions changed, so, strangely, we were actually left for several minutes completely alone. I felt bathed, uplifted, in the love Francis had for all living creatures, and indeed for all living nature. I felt I could understand the loving gaze with which he looked across the valley from the hermitage, greeting brother tree, brother wolf, brother wind and sun. This was not an emotional love but a true, creative vision. It enabled him to see into the invisible. And as we know it enabled him to bring peace between man and animal, and oppressor and oppressed.

'On his day (October 4th) let us trust in the closeness of a brother whose heart reached out to embrace everything! I think we will hear his radiant song and feel his gift.'

Ylana also wrote some lovely words about the stone circle at Castlerigg, in England's Lake District.

'I walked slowly around the circle stopping to put my hand on the individual stones, as I love to do. When I came to stand right in the centre of the circle I was aware that, behind the bright physical sunlight, there seemed to be a golden light arising from the earth. At the same time there was a beautiful warm radiance shining down into the centre of the circle. I can still see it!

'With my eyes closed, the circle of stones felt like a receptacle, even a chalice. I felt how there was a radiation outwards of peace and gentle strength from this receptacle. I could not tell how far this emanation spread but I knew it was truly a manifestation of the 'ancient spiritual fire' in the heart of Britain.'

A Final Word

THE LIGHT IN BRITAIN ended with this inspiring inner pilgrimage, guiding the reader on a journey of discovery.

Ivan Cooke is our guide and looks back to the saintliness
of men and women who long predate Christian saints.

'Again we stand in fancy, you and I, on some height far
above the prevailing earthiness; say, on a chalk down wide
in expanse. Our feeling of height is due to its purity, to
an abiding peace, to its wholesomeness and holiness. We
stand beside a low earthen mound, once a burial place
for some sainted man or woman. His bones are now dust,
but holy dust, impregnated with himself; and all the air
around, and all the ethers, the flowers, the birds, the little creatures, they too know about the sainted one and in
their way they worship.

'Let us assume we stand on Maiden Castle, a wide expanse of downland guarded by banks and entrenchments,
all erected since our saint's time, who knew none of these
things. Neither did his people in the long ago. A thousand
years, two, five thousand years – these are but insignifi-
cant periods of time which flee past our sainted man like
dream days; while as they fly, his essence remains because
he and such as he are fathers to our Britain, and we are his
sons who inherited his rich estate.

'Somehow, we respond, we react. It comes to us as a
wondrous feeling; so that we want to embrace, to hold the
very soil close to ourselves.

'The day is fine, warm and dry. Now we lie stretched at
full length upon the short turf, trodden these many thousand years past by human feet; and as we lie the savour
of it reaches down into us, deeply, full of rustlings and
the runnings of tiny creatures. We bury our face in sweet
grass; and then most wondrously, our heaviness of body
departs. Our coat-of-skin thins away. We feel no longer

boxed-down in flesh, but are lightened, illumined by a kind of luminous ether. We feel, we know that were we so inclined we could leap and run high and fast as never men have done before, that we are become light and ageless. Yet heaviness and ageing still wait like a bad dream in our background – this also we know, while feeling still above and beyond such heaviness.

'Now have our senses also become finer, rarer; we are aware as never before of how close are the little people. They rustle and cluster around us now, prying, peeping, all-an-itch with curiosity. We do not take them too closely to ourselves, do not give out too much, lest we dissipate our nerve force, our soul force. Instead, we go deeper within.

'Then we forget all else, even this Edenic land our souls have reached, and in which we momentarily live. For now a power comes such as we have no words to describe, but can only feel as a glowing inflow of life. It seems to fill all earth and the skies above, reaching out to, pervading, quickening all things – indeed, hushing all troublous, clamouring thoughts until silence itself becomes quickened with its glory and wonder.

'Then do we know but one truth only, one truth surely; that there be neither death nor evil ruling in this world of ours, that neither can endure. That all creation works towards life eternal, life enduring, everlasting. In this certitude we rest. In this surpassing surety we abide, all problems solved at last.'

PART FOUR

Exploring Sacred Places with White Eagle

Let us now follow White Eagle as he leads us to some of the specific centres of power he has talked about, the places in our world that have great spiritual significance. With White Eagle as our guide, as pilgrims we explore the quiet and sacred places, the mountains, the ancient buildings and temples.

WE HAVE BEEN speaking about the ancient mysteries, the ancient peoples of the earth. Why are you all attracted by this interesting subject? Is it because your mind is searching for fresh material, or is it because there is a note of memory struck in your soul-consciousness? This ancient knowledge speaks through the innermost voice of the heart. As the present race begins to awaken spiritually, it will learn to read in stones and in the earth's formation the histories of its ancient peoples. It will learn the inner secret of how the wise beings of the past built not only the temples (of which only a few remain) but also the spiritual life of men and women, which has been sustained ever since. It is not only a building with material stones which has been going on since the beginning of time, but a building of the spiritual power and the life essences in earth and in humanity.

The mystery schools established in the beginning have continued throughout the world's history, extending to one continent after another. Inscriptions on relics of stone still testifying to the existence of these schools can be found, but the modern investigator does not yet comprehend their meaning. Nor does the modern mind understand one iota of the power and glory and truth still impregnated in these stones, in the very earth – because this truth is hidden in the Sun itself. As surely as the Sun's rays penetrate the earth and all physical matter and life, so this ancient wisdom and this mystery of life still impregnates all matter with its divine origin.

The earth seems a dark place at the moment, but never forget that all physical and material atoms are yet impregnated with divine truth, this spiritual sunlight. Without it the world would disintegrate, and all life be withdrawn from this planet.

What we have to say about our ancient brethren comes to us from the depths of spirit consciousness. We are not in a position to quote books or ancient manuscripts. We can only bring forth deep truths from the spirit but are assured that all that we say can be corroborated by evidence written in nature – in the stones, in the formation of the land, in relics of past races which will be brought to the surface for study. We beg you to understand the importance of not being too definite in the realm of mysticism, else you may divert others from truth. Be very comprehensive. White Eagle believes in everything, because he knows there is truth in everything – lying beneath the clothing with which humanity likes to dress it up. We deal with our subject solely from the inner aspect and ask you not to try to correlate our words with outer evidences, for confusion will result if you do.

Truth lies within every soul. Each one's vision varies according to their evolution.

The religion brought to the earth millions of years ago is a religion not on the lips but in the heart. I see in the future, temples, or sanctified places to which the new brotherhoods are drawn ... shall we say, sanctified centres of grace and power, wherein men and women can worship the Lord their God, not with lips but with the outpouring of hearts, and the drawing to themselves of creative forces, and the utilization of those forces for the gradual perfecting or growth of all forms of life.

The Quiet and Sacred Places

To get near to heaven, leave the lowlands and climb a hill, or better still, a mountain. There are a number of holy mountains in different parts of the earth. Think for a moment about this; it is natural to go up a mountain to seek light, to seek peace. You want to raise your consciousness away from the plains, away from the depths; to the heights you naturally aspire. In the heights, in the mountaintops, live tranquillity and peace. The eagle – symbol of the bird of vision! Only through spiritual vision (does not the soaring eagle see the whole earth laid bare beneath?), from the heights, or the mountains, and from the quiet and sacred places, can truth stand revealed.

On the mountains there are the great angels, almost lesser gods. Certain mountains are sacred, and these great angels guard the sacred place, enthroned on the Holy Mountains of the West, the East, the North and the South. I do not think that humanity will ever break through such a guard. Where the adepts and masters live remains undiscovered. A certain mountain in Wales, called, I think, Cader Idris, is a place of power, for on this mountain certain magical rites were performed. In Ireland is a centre, a holy mountain, the place of residence of one of the masters. We remember the holy mountain in the Andes, where another little band of White Brethren settled.* In other words, those men and women to whom were entrusted the mysteries, fled or retired – perhaps to the Himalayas or the Andes, the secret and sacred caves, where the record of the mysteries is still preserved.

It is noticeable how frequently the mountaintop is referred to in connection with the Masters, with groups and lodges. There are a number of holy mountains in different parts of the earth where assemble the Brethren whose work it is to watch over the progress and spiritual growth of mankind. In such places these advanced souls who are called Masters or Elder Brethren live and work. At certain times of the year there is a common meeting ground. Remember that these Elder Brothers are not confined or limited by time or space, and can travel in a flash to any point on your earth. There they gather in a grand ceremony to further their work and to project the rays of light and truth into groups and countries working for the good of humankind, and also into the hearts of individuals.

*See p. 24 for the White or Star Brotherhood.

Inner Pilgrimage to the Mountaintops

Long ago we perambulated the great mountain places in prayer and silence except for the rhythmic tread of human feet. We recommend you to go right up into the mountains. Be alone, listening; observe the life of nature, and from outward recognition and realization of the universal life, look inwards.

Remember that countless numbers of white brethren have circled the temple of the White Brotherhood in the wide open spaces on the mountaintop.... Become one with this brotherhood in the heavens, aware of the stars, of the air, of the moonlight and the coming dawn ... and the sunlight. Feel the beauty of the wings of the eagle in your own heart, feel the carpet of flowers at your feet, hear the song of the birds of the night and of the morning; hear the wind in the pine trees...

We would raise your consciousness from your physical body to the spiritual worlds, and would ask you to concentrate upon the mountains in the East, the dawn of the sun, the rising sun and the stillness of the vast mountains. Let us rise together to the mountaintops, far above the noise and clamour of the world. In thought we will go on wings to the mountain, the holy mountain capped with golden light.... The light from the holy mountain goes forth to bathe the mystic isle.... Visualize the vast snow-capped peaks bathed in the golden sunlight.

In the silence, on the mountaintop, with the canopy of heaven's peace spread over us and the stars of the eternal wisdom to guide us, we worship the grandeur and glory of our Creator's handiwork and, becoming in tune with the infinite Spirit, we awaken to the beauty within ourselves. We feel the beauty, the peace, and the eternal love of our Father God.

Where Ceremonies have Taken Place

There are many centres of power, places which have received concentrated rays of God power. We will divide these centres of power into two classes, and in the first group place those which have been the subject of magical practices at different times, centres where such great men as masters have stayed, resided, worked, taught. We mean centres from which such great ones have passed onwards, leaving the physical vehicle that they used. It need not necessarily be a full master, but a great initiate; a highly advanced soul may leave that benediction of wonderful power and light behind. A master more often than not takes his physical body away – but that is another subject.

At certain places in your own country great souls have left the physical body. A master today may not necessarily have attained mastership some centuries ago. In the particular place where he then died, he left a body; that place is now sanctified, a place of power. The power of attraction would still draw the power of the master to where the personality is revered and perhaps the tomb of his former incarnation preserved.

Secondly we class such places as cathedrals and buildings, which are the subject of human thought and concentration, as places of power too. Where humanity gathers, it concentrates thought-power, not necessarily of very great value. In other words, a building becomes saturated with the aura of those who continually visit it, resulting in a degree of power or emanation from the substance of the building.

When you walk among ruins, strive to attune yourself to the inner vibrations. Great ceremonies have been enacted in places which now lie in ruins. Go to the building, alone if possible, raise your consciousness and you will receive much. Those of you who are developing this inner vision, if you visit these places you will see these things for yourselves, see their ceremonies, see their mode of life. Those ceremonies still live in the ether and can be seen. All comes to life again.

We will tell you of certain centres of power which many of you have visited and therefore are of particular interest. There are centres in the mystic Isle of Britain where a great, a perfect light has been accumulating for centuries – centres where long ago sincere and holy brethren met to practise the mysteries. Upon them a blazing golden light poured down, and through them it impregnated the very earth itself. All these centres are in turn linked with certain centres in Europe and Asia and across again to America – there is also a spiritual centre in the Andes – indeed, they exist all round the world.

Deep Truths Written in the Stones

Deep truths from the spirit are written in nature – in the stones, in the formation of the land. Stones have within them a spiritual power and life. The great and wise ones brought the full power of the spiritual sun, whose very stones were impregnated with light, to spread gradually over the northern hemisphere and right across the equator to the south. The ancients thought they had discovered the life spirit, in the stone. They thought they had found the life – the spark – the fire. Have you ever heard of lights found burning in closed caves in the secret places of the earth, lights which have remained burning through the centuries? Little lights have been discovered in your own country and all over the world, and are buried within the stones.

Stones and stone circles were set up by the ancients as a representation of their ideal of God. Arranged in circles, the stones were thought to give the idea of the encircling power, the protective power of God, and also the idea of God as the Source of all life. The ancients left upon the stones language, markings, which reveal the inner wonders of life to any who can read the language of the Gods. Being ignorant of the spiritual life, people are unable to interpret the symbols and markings on the ancient stones. As the present race begins to awaken spiritually, it will learn to read in stones and in the earth's formation the histories of its ancient peoples. Spiritual power will tell you which stones were so used and which were not, for if you stand by them your soul will know.

When you visit places where these mystical stones and mounds are to be found, remember they are impregnated with the spiritual forces of the divine fire of the white magic. Some of the ancient stone circles were temples of sun worship, for the worship of the whole heavens, and for the study of astronomy. There are many of these in Britain, such as the stone circles at Stonehenge and Avebury, but in many places in Europe and in America and in the East too – indeed in every continent – you find monoliths, great stones. Sometimes they stand singly, sometimes in groups. Your stone monuments can be found in England, in Scotland, and in the islands around Scotland – in Brittany, elsewhere in Europe, in India, in Egypt, in ancient America, in the Andes and in the Gobi desert. Ireland still contains the remnants of temples of sun worship. There are many such ancient centres in Ireland. Others exist in remoter parts, and others in France, and in South America as well as in India. There is still much conjecture about the temple at Avebury, about the monuments on the chalk downs of England, about the temple at Stonehenge on the great plain, and about the dolmens and stone circles in Cornwall, and about other centres and places of power and magic on the west coast in Wales and Scotland. Let us speak from what we know.

Stonehenge

Little is known to history about Stonehenge. But the soul who can penetrate the veil of matter will note an accord between the position of the stones and those of the sun and planets. The stones at Stonehenge mark the place where cosmic or planetary rays meet. People will learn that there are these points all over the British Isles where there was a concentration of planetary rays, and at such points – like the chakras of the light of this mystic isle – there is a tremendous spiritual impetus and inspiration.

On such a spot you will find enormous spiritual and psychic force. Great ceremonies of initiation will have taken place there, initiations of those now passed away from the earth cycle. If you go to Stonehenge at certain times and open your inner vision (have a few dreams, you know!) you will see there beings who are sometimes described as angels. They are the ancient ones. When a soul of vision visits this sun temple their eyes are opened and they see how great angels come close, drawn back to the scene of former ceremonies. The ancient brotherhood is still there and still enacting a grand cosmic ceremony year by year.

When a soul is attuned to the etheric influence of the stones, when it is attuned to the agelessness of life, it is able to see enacted there a great and glorious heavenly scene, a vast company of angelic beings gathered, protecting the holy light. They watch the ceremony. They see the rays of the heavenly light directed upon the altar, the sacred stone. That ceremony is as old as creation, as old as life itself on this earth. The brethren participating in it are invisible, they come to help humanity. They come to bring light, to stimulate light in the stones on your earth.

An Inner Pilgrimage to Stonehenge

Open your vision…. You will be able to see enacted there a great and glorious heavenly scene. Is it on earth or is it in heaven? You are part of it; and the first thing that you, the soul, sees is a vast company of angels: the great ceremony of the angels encircling and marching. You will see the most beautiful movement, hear the tone and sound of the music of the heavens, and the great paean of praise which goes forth … you will hear the very creative power and the Word which is being used.

See this vast company of angelic beings gathered there, protecting this holy light. Remember, we speak of the light buried in the stone, buried in earth. As surely as the Sun's rays penetrate the earth and all physical matter, so the light of the ancient wisdom still impregnates the stones and the earth about them.

See the first rays of the sun strike that Rose Stone. The brothers of the rose, brothers of the ancient light, are there as well. They make no claims. The greater the brother, the more silent is he or she. Flowing from that heart there is ever love, love, love, kindness, goodwill; the brother sees always God, always good.

You are the stones; these great ones come to help you; they bring indescribable spiritual power and love.

Avebury

Many temples stand as a symbol of the worship of the earth and the heavens. The stones which were once scattered over Britain are to be seen reassembled at Avebury in Wiltshire, where is another temple. This temple, we believe, was originally some miles in length and formed of immense stones with, in the centre, a great circle. The temple was open to the sun, and in its centre was a raised altar. Such an altar was not built facing east as today. The people would gather around its base and on the top the fire ceremony was conducted. At these ceremonies the priests, assisted by the great beings from other planets, worked magic. You know little about this magic today, but then it was much in evidence.

A long approach or avenue leads you today to what was the centre of the great temple of Avebury. Some miles away are still to be found stones indicating the path the ancients trod as they went to worship. Following the avenue, the approach to that temple takes the form of the serpent, which suggests the temple having originated from serpent worship. This, you must remember, is worship not of the actual reptile but of that symbolic serpent which lies curled at the base of the human spine. We mean of course the power of kundalini, which is the latent spiritual creative force in humanity. Those who have knowledge of the unfoldment of psychic and spiritual power will know that this kundalini, like a serpent sleeping at the base of the spine, can be raised up into the higher consciousness of man–woman, to be used for creating good in the world.

The serpent stands for wisdom and knowledge, which wisdom comes to humanity with the rising of this spiritual essence within himself.

Carnac

There is another temple in Brittany at Carnac. Some of the stones there were carved in the form of the human being, sometimes the form of animals, and sometimes in the form of a great eagle, which was then considered a symbol of flight, a symbol of vision. It also had the two aspects of good and evil, for while the eagle could soar into the heavens it could also sweep down to destroy its prey. That was a reminder of the dual aspects of the deity – a very important lesson which humans have yet to absorb and which many at present reject.

We are referring to the dual aspects of God – the creative and the destructive. Where there is creation and evolution, there must be an outbreathing, and there must also be an inbreathing. With creation there must also be destruction – the clearing away and absorbing of that which has been disassembled. You cannot have the creative aspect without the destructive – or the power of absorption and redistribution, if you like to put it that way.

People think that God is wholly good. True, God is wholly good if you can once see the purpose of what appears to be destructive. See how wide the vision must be before the truth of life can be understood! In the symbols which the ancients used in their worship, in their religion, can be traced these esoteric truths of life. Until such symbols are rightly understood they are likely to remain enigmas to humankind.

America

The original stone worship and the following sun worship is to be found in all countries. The oldest, we think, is in America, for America (particularly the southern half) has best withstood the ravages of nature, and parts of America have not been submerged like practically every other portion of the earth at some time or another. These same early temples of stone in America have yet to be uncovered.

From the West the knowledge was taken to the East. We know that there is a saying that in the East the sun rises and the light comes. That is true in one sense. But it was from what you call the western hemisphere, from South America, that the priests first set forth carrying with them their religion of sun worship, and more – the inner secrets of the life in the spirit realms as well as the life of the spirit as manifested through matter.

In America, and we speak of things we remember, our brethren used naturally the knowledge of the priests in the temples of the White Light ... the temples which were erected on high places, never in the valleys ... the temples themselves erected by the white magic. The stones forming these temples, often weighing many hundreds of tons, were placed by those called priests of the Plumed Serpent, because they had the full development of the divine fires within their consciousness.

The stones were very sacred to our people, because they contained holy elements, attracted from more radiant and more evolved planets. Such stones were used to receive the bodies of those who died. This is perhaps new to you. The holy stones, and altars in the white temples, in Atlantis and in ancient America, were recipients of the bodies of the dead. The body was consumed, or absorbed, into the holy stones, its components disintegrated and returned into the elements from which they came. We could talk to you so much, so very much, about these things....

Buildings of Heavenly Power

There are many buildings of worship, and they are pregnant with power, and will attract the traveller, the mystic and the student. An abbey, cathedral or temple is a building erected to the glory of God, a fit house in which to worship the Creator. Whenever a great ceremony has been performed, whether in a church or on a hilltop, it leaves an impression on the surrounding ether which never fades and can be again celebrated in the etheric world.

In a church – or anywhere where ritual is used – ritual can produce very great power. If your eyes were opened to the inner vision you would see whorls of light, almost like illumined smoke, and you would see these forces whirling round and round and building into etheric pillars of light, sometimes of exquisite beauty. Very often it is where there has been in the past ritual which has built this spiritual power.

Glastonbury – and St Albans

The centre known as Glastonbury: is it merely a ruin? Of course you know better! You know it as a centre of exceptional power, not only that which is concentrated there from past ceremonies, but because of power rays at present being concentrated there for future revelation. British mysteries are to be found buried in the sacred precincts of the ancient abbey of Glastonbury. Here lie the bones of a master. Buried there are relics of power, relics of power simply because they were used in certain practices, certain Christian ceremonies of Great Britain.

Glastonbury was the centre of a very early Christian Brotherhood. He who is known as Joseph of Arimathea visited your country, travelled from the East to the West and rested at various places. Where he rested, the spot was impregnated with certain power rays.

When you walk among the ruins at Glastonbury, strive to attune yourself to the inner vibrations. Reconstruct in your imagination the grand abbey which was built upon that holy ground by the universal architects, by those who held a knowledge now lost; not merely of construction, but of symmetry, proportion, vibration, and a spiritual knowledge. If you walk into what is called the Joseph Chapel, towards the altar, there you will encounter a tremendous power. Enter the main building and look towards the higher altar, and again you will feel this concentration. You will perhaps hear singing, one of the first things you are likely to contact, since the whole atmosphere is impregnated with the vibrations of music, because of the ceremonies which were there performed.

Outside the town of Glastonbury is a hill called the Tor. No ordinary person understands the extraordinary power concentrated on that spot, the result of certain

magical rites performed by the druids, which left a chain of magical power that will remain for centuries unbroken.

Many have visited the Abbey of St Alban; if you have not, put it on your list. I select this place for a reason. You cannot fail to register the power and spiritual beauty, not only of the building itself, but the whole town; the very ground can appear sanctified. He who was once known as St Alban is greater than generally supposed, and is now one of a group of masters closely associated with the spiritual reconstruction now taking place. The body used is buried in the cathedral. Remember this, and find out more. Go to the shrine, alone if possible, raise your consciousness and you will receive much.

Ancient Temples

Many temples stand as a symbol of the worship of the earth and the heavens. These temples were the outward expression of an inner spiritual wisdom; the builders were themselves initiates of the ancient wisdom, and brought into action all the powers of the soul in their creations. Every part of the structure of these ancient buildings was in due harmony with the planetary influences; each part built as an expression of the grand harmonies of the universe.

From their teachers the people learnt the wisdom, the secrets of what is called 'magic'. They were taught to use the spiritual powers of the Christ within,* to build their

---

*Every man, woman and child on earth has within their being a 'light' to guide them. White Eagle calls this the Christ spirit, the spirit of divine love. The word 'Christ' is meant universally, and should not be linked with any particular religion.

temples of worship. They did not build as you understand building, but were true operative masons, possessing the secret of drawing to the earth certain forces, rays of life-force, and invisible elements which when drawn to the earth consolidated, and formed into certain stones. This was the true masonry. You will wonder at this, and think that masonry is applied only to the spiritual aspect of life. But this was also the spiritual to the brothers in those days. This, my brethren, was the origin of temples, the remnants of which are still to be found in Britain and other parts of the world.

These great temples were erected before time, as you understand time, and by great initiates. They represent the foundation of a religion – indeed, more a science of life, pertaining not particularly to the life physical, but to the whole plan of the soul's evolution. Nothing less can be found in these mighty temples – earthly monuments they are, but for those sufficiently quickened in spiritual perception to read and to understand as something greater.

Many of you retain memories of previous incarnations. The memories of life since our creation lie within us and it only requires a certain chord or vibration to touch that memory for it to be brought to the consciousness. Thus many of us have memories of temples in the past and of hearing from the silence the command, 'Let the light shine!'

The monuments of which we speak were primarily temples of initiation, so that the candidates, working within, would absorb the invisible influences. This would draw to their souls the vibrations which would stimulate their soul qualities; vibrations which would, in due order, help them to open the centres of light within their own temple ... the temple of their body.

Pyramids, Temples of Initiation

A pyramid is not only a lasting monument but a temple of light, a temple of initiation. It contains all the lesser secrets of our being, and also the greater mysteries of the heavens, and of past and future ages. It was not built by any ordinary means. It was a creation accomplished by the priests of the white light, literally built through spiritual or heavenly power.

The pyramid contains all the secrets of God, and indicates the path which every child of God has to take on its journey from the source to the very end. The complete life is symbolized in the Great Pyramid – the life built upon a square. The square is a symbol of humanity, and the character has to be made perfect and true before it can fit into the building of the temple in the heavens; all the knocks and the difficulties, the pain and the suffering of human life, are the blows which the rough stone receives in the process of making it smooth and perfect, so that it will fit perfectly into the divine temple that is being built in the heavens by the race or life cycle to which it belongs.

The pyramid goes down into the sands to a greater depth than it rises above the earth. Each side of the pyramid is a triangle, reminding us that our aspirations must go upward to the apex. The sun shines upon all four sides of the pillar, all four triangles. By the four is meant the great outpouring of the spiritual sun during all four seasons of the year. The spiritual sun enables humanity to receive that spiritual help and stimulation without which they must fail to reach their goal.

As it was a temple of initiation, the glories a pyramid contains can only be revealed to the initiate. As the soul becomes raised in degree after degree in these spiritual mysteries, so it will learn more and see more the wonder, the perfection, of that temple of stone. And it will remain as it is until the truth it contains is revealed, or is discovered. Not only do the very stones themselves and the shape and form of such a building contain great esoteric truths, but chambers within that building hold written records in stone, telling of the beginning of life on this earth, records of all that has happened, of the rise and fall of races and continents.

Many have sought to unlock the secret contained in the Great Pyramid of Giza. The House of Light was the name given to the Great Pyramid, and the candidate to the inner mysteries sought wisdom and knowledge through entering. It is not the tomb of kings, a place of mortality; but rather the birthplace of the King in humankind. For the soul entered, through secret chambers concealed without the precincts, into the secret, inner chambers of the mysteries, not only of the stone building, but of the candidate's own temple, their own nature.

Great pyramids are not only to be found in Egypt, where they are best known; there are others that remain a mystery awaiting discovery. The Great Pyramid contains not only the secrets of the earth, but of eternal life. In these temples human beings were initiated and taught, or their own souls revealed – as a result of certain forms and ceremonies – the purpose of their creation. In the pyramid they learnt whence they came, for what they were then living, and whither they went.

In Central America there are ruins of many temples and pyramids. There is one particular pyramid that still stands there. We would like to convey to you, if we can, something of the atmosphere of this pyramid. Picture a large ceremonial hall, the walls of this hall lined with gold. In the east of this Lodge there were seven steps leading to a throne of gold, of exquisite workmanship; the delicacy of the tracing upon this throne was beyond work of your present age. Picture the great silence, because that was a feature of the Hall of Initiation – silence. It felt as though we were in the immensity of eternity.

The Magic Island of Iona

Some of the isles of the Hebrides are actually the summits of islands and mountains whereon were established the holy temples of the White Light. The heart of that is the blessed isle of Iona. Little is known as yet of Iona but its

fame has begun to spread, and for this reason. By contrast you can visit the great temples in Egypt, the Andes,
India or Tibet, and still examine the grandeur of their
structure, the nobility of the buildings. All these centres
speak of grandeur and age, but on the physical or material plane. They are material symbols which the intellectual
can study with keen interest and wonder. But when we
go to that little jewel cradled in the ocean, Iona, the sun
shines and the light rises from its very ground.

On that isle of the blessed we become aware of tremendous age-old power but also of a gentleness, a beauty
unsurpassed, of the deep peace and purity of that place.
Something is there in the rock of Iona which is eternal
beauty, purity and peace. That is the difference between
the little isle of the blessed and the temples of Egypt. In
the latter you once had the pomp of high civilization. In
the former you find the pulse of God still beating.

When you go to Iona you become aware of tremendous age-old power, but also of a gentleness, a beauty
unsurpassed, of the deep peace and purity of that place.
On that sacred island set in the green sea there exists,
within the earth, the crumbled stones of a temple which
was a place of initiation ... a temple of the white light.
This ancient temple, where the Masters lived, in course
of time was swept away, but there remain on Iona etheric impressions of the lives of the ancient brothers and
it attracts, even today, angelic forces. Those who have
eyes to see, who have ears to hear the angelic brethren
and the nature spirits of Iona, will see and will hear the
impression on the etheric. Do not think however that the
presence of forms of bygone days, or shall we call them

etheric memories, or spirit impressions, are the actual spirits of those who lived long ago. But there certainly remain on Iona etheric impressions of the lives of some of the ancient brothers.

The magic of Iona rests with the very stones of the island. The power which was brought down from the heavens and drawn to Iona has impregnated the very rocks.

Something is there in the rock of Iona which is eternal beauty, purity and peace. And the power which was brought down from the heavens, and drawn to Iona as a result of the masonic ritual practised to such a fine degree, has impregnated the very rocks. We believe that there remains in Iona a special stone which was the original creation of the master masons, a stone which was formed by the true and perfect ritual, the ceremonies which the ancient brothers worked long ago. You know what we mean by this: a masonic stone which was formed by the true and perfect ritual, the ceremonies that the ancient brothers worked long ago. This is the power still to be felt, and the power which will call back the brothers again to Iona, to rebuild the temple of light.

Inner Pilgrimage to the Temple of Light

We would give you a picture, a symbol if you like, of a temple. No printed or painted picture can convey the same idea as an actual temple, the creation of one's mind and soul. Will you open your soul to the reception of rays of light from the world of light?

Close your eyes and forget your personal self, your material conditions and surroundings. Ascend the spiral of light which rises up to the heavens, up and up and up....

Think as though you are approaching a vast temple of light and beautiful colour ... and that through the pillars of this temple you can see across a vista of flowers and blue water and beyond, to mountains capped with golden light and rising into the sunlight. Enter into this temple. Come with us into this temple of the spirit. Open the eyes of your soul. Let your heavenly, your higher imagination help you to see the beauty of this place of worship and of brotherhood. Feel as well as see; see that you are in the midst of a shining company of brothers and sisters of the ancient white light.... Then you will see clearly the great white temple of the spirit.

See with your mind's eye the grandeur and the beauty of this arched temple, vast and yet enclosing us in such a way that although we are able to realize the vastness and the sense of the universal in this temple, we are at the same time united as a company of brothers and sisters. See the groups of elder brethren encircling us. Such harmony exists between us that we do not feel at a loss in a strange and vast place, but as one; we are a group of brothers of the light. We would like you all to become more conscious of these elder brethren and of their help in forwarding the plan created in the heavens for the evolution of humankind. In your mind's eye you may see that we are in a temple similar in shape to an Egyptian temple, the roof supported by many pillars; but its main beauty is the golden light which floods it, a radiance emanating from the temple itself. It appears to stream in great power from a central point in the canopy above. In these rays of golden light we see many exquisite colours: the seven primary colours which we know and many others of great beauty. Mount the seven steps to the golden altar, the blazing block of gold, behind which is a lighted window. Visualize this, gaze upon it with all your soul, absorb the essence of this golden light....

There is silence in this temple. Then a voice. We cannot see the speaker, but the command rings through our temple: 'Let the Light Shine!'

To Be a Pilgrim

A group of pilgrims were searching for a master, one who was said to have great wisdom, one who would help them to find heaven. In due course, after a long and troublesome journey, they found themselves before a cave in the mountainside, in which the one who was said to be a master was seated in meditation. After a time of preparation, they were invited to enter the presence of the holy man. He remained in meditation as they entered; no word was spoken. But when they were seated, he raised his face;

and they saw shining, not only from his face, but from his whole being, a glorious light which penetrated their own beings, until they felt that their bodies and the very clothing they wore were alight, blazing, even as was the light which they saw in the master's aura. They absorbed his beauty and were bathed in the glory of the heavenly light.

This is a simple illustration of what it is expected that you, individually, will give to humankind as you unfold. It is hoped that one day you will become so impregnated with the holiness and love of the Master that you will carry His–Her gentleness and love out into the world. Is it asking too much? It is difficult for you, we know, for the world may appear cruel and hard, but it is peopled with a suffering humanity and those who appear cruel and hard, as you would describe them, are truly in need of the light which you can carry them. Not only are you a vessel of light, even as a little lamp burning on the altar, but you may relight the lamp of your brother, your sister.

[From the book, THE LIGHT BRINGER]

Finding the Holy Grail

Before we cease may we tell you of the scene now with you. For the knights are seated at the table spread with the pure white cloth. In the centre is the Holy Grail, which is lifted up by perfect hands.... Come with us in spirit, and we will try to describe to you this mystical bowl of light. Can you see revealed on the horizon this gradually expanding and rising bowl of light, the cup of the Holy Grail, symbol of a more glorious life?

To you, my brother and sister, the Holy Grail is offered. This is no fantasy, but the greatest reality that one can ever know – the reception into his hands of this magic cup, the Holy Grail which all souls are seeking, though they know not what they seek.

Take it – now. From it flows a living fountain which never ceases. It is your life, but also eternal life. And the Holy Grail is fashioned as the human heart. The human heart is the cup, the grail cup. The law is love, and love is justice. Love is wisdom. Love is gentleness. Love is power. Let there be love.

APPENDIX 1

The Tree of Light Breathing Routine

This is a simple breathing routine which, in a sense, combines everything – meditation and sending out the light, breathing, and so on – so that if there is time for no more than this in a busy day you can still feel spiritually and physically refreshed and stretched and have shared a blessing by sending out the light.

Begin by standing, if possible, facing an open window or beautiful view. Feel your feet on the ground. Close your eyes and take a few gentle, deep, relaxed breaths just to calm your mind and help you to focus it upon the shining Star. Next, take a big sigh, let all worries go, and relax. Now let your head fall forward, your arms too, and feel utterly deflated, like a balloon with no air in it. Now, breathe in slowly, gently, deeply, filling yourself with the life-force, the breath of God from the Sun; do this as you gradually straighten, raising your arms sideways, stretching them as wide as possible, and lean slightly back; and complete the inhalation as you stretch up, up, up towards the Sun, reaching as high as you can, until your hands meet above your head.

Hold this for a moment or two, revelling in being filled with light. As you breathe out, bring the light down through your whole body, suiting the action to the thought by cupping the light in your two hands, as though holding a Star, the light from which touches head and throat and heart centres as your hands slowly return to your sides. As you bring your hands right down, feel that the light they have brought from the Sun is passing right down into Mother Earth beneath your feet, to bless and enrich her. Repeat this cycle a minimum of three times. Think: 'Divine Light shines in me ... Divine Light floods and fills every atom of my being....'

Now, reverse the process and from the original position, stretch your toes again and stretch your fingers too, towards the earth. Think of your body as a tree of light, its roots in the earth, its branches reaching towards the Sun. And as you breathe in, draw the life-force from the earth up through your body (the trunk of the tree, all light). Your arms, this time, are not spread wide as they were before. Your hands, with fingertips together as in prayer, pass slowly up the trunk, drawing up the life-force and again reaching right into the Sun, stretching heavenwards with praise and thanksgiving to God. You are offering into the heart of God all that you have and are.

Again hold the fully stretched position for a moment or two, and then on the outbreath spread the arms wide, wide, wide in blessing. They are the branches of a great tree of light spread wide as the world. As you gradually lower your arms with the outbreath, you are radiating light from your heart and your whole being, enfolding humankind and all creation in the light. This cycle too should be repeated a minimum of three times. Or, if you prefer, you can alternate the two routines, but always end with the one in which you send out the light. Finally, take two or three more gentle breaths, holding the invisible Star to your heart and again gently breathing out its blessing.

APPENDIX 2

Sacred Places Mentioned in this Book

The Apostles: A collection of limestone stacks off the shore of the Port Campbell National Park, by the Great Ocean Road in Victoria, Australia.

Avebury: A Neolithic henge monument containing three stone circles, in Wiltshire, England. Avebury contains the largest stone circle in Europe.

Cader Idris: just one of

Carnac: The Carnac stone alignments are one of the largest Neolithic menhir collections in the world, located near Vannes, Brittany, France.

Chartres Cathedral: A medieval 'Roman Rite' Catholic cathedral in the department of Eure-et-Loire, France, about 80 kilometres (50 miles) southwest of Paris.

Edfu, Egypt: The Temple of Horus at Edfu is the most completely preserved of all the temple remains in Egypt. Edfu is a city on the west bank of the Nile River between Esna and Aswan.

English Downland. The chalk folds that comprise the downland (from a Celtic word for 'hills') extend across southern England from Kent to Somerset, and from central southern England, ancient Wessex, up to the Norfold coast. They are rich in ancient monuments, most of all at their approximate centre, which includes the Avebury complex of monuments and (also mentioned here) those around Uffington. *The Great Ridgeway* runs across this central section, too.

Ephesus, Turkey: An ancient Greek city and later a major Roman city, on the coast of Ionia, near present-day Selçuk, Izmir Province, Turkey.

Glastonbury: A small town in Somerset, England, notable for myths and legends often related to Glastonbury Tor and Glastonbury Abbey. Among others, the legends have to do with Joseph of Arimathea, the Holy Grail and King Arthur.

The Great Barrier Reef: The world's largest coral reef system, off the coast of Queensland, Australia.

Great Pyramid, Giza: Oldest and largest of the three pyramids at Giza, Egypt; one of the seven wonders of the ancient world.

The Himalaya: mountain range in Asia separating the plains of the Indian subcontinent from the Tibetan Plateau. They contain the highest mountains in the world, including Everest, which is called *Qomolungma* (Goddess Mother of the Snows) in Chinese and *Sagarmatha* in contemporary Nepali.

Iona: A small island in the Inner Hebrides off the Ross of Mull on the western coast of Scotland, and – in more recent times than some of those described – the site of the first monastic foundation by St Columba. It is crowned by the hill known as Dun-I.

Lhasa, Tibet: Tibet is a plateau region in Asia, northeast of the Himalayas. The traditional homeland of the Tibetan people and the highest region on earth. Lhasa is the highest city in the world and contains many important Buddhist sites.

Lightning Ridge: A town in New South Wales, Australia, known for its fossils and opals.

Lordat: A hilltop village in the department of Ariège, France, which has possible connections with the Cathars; the area was particularly important in the Cathar revival of 1295–1310.

Machu Picchu: fifteenth-century Inca site in Peru, located high in the mountains and often referred to as the 'Lost City of the Incas'.

Machapuchare: mountain in the Annapurna Himal of north central Nepal. It is seen as particularly sacred and has never been climbed to the summit.

Maiden Castle: An Iron Age hill fort two miles south west of Dorchester, Dorset, England.

Montségur: Refuge of the Cathars in the thirteenth century, it was besieged and fell in March 1244. The bulk of those inside were burned at the stake in the pass beneath.

Newgrange, County Meath: A prehistoric monument in County Meath, Ireland, about one kilometre north of the River Boyne. It is possibly older even than Stonehenge and the Egyptian pyramids.

Pic de St-Barthélèmy: Also known as the Montagne de Tabe, this is the outlier of the Pyrenees that sits between Montségur (q.v.) and Lordat.

Ring of Brodgar, Orkney: A Neolithic henge and stone circle on the Mainland, the largest island in Orkney, Scotland.

Rosslyn Chapel: Chapel at Roslin in Midlothian, Scotland, often associated with the Knights Templar.

Stonehenge: A prehistoric monument in Wiltshire, England, eight miles north of Salisbury. The Stonehenge visible today is the remains of a larger monument still, and at the heart of an area more rich in prehistoric sites than almost anywhere known.

Tintagel: A village and castle on the Atlantic coast of Cornwall, associated with King Arthur.

Uffington, Oxfordshire, complex of monuments. On the borders of Oxfordshire, Wiltshire and Berkshire, England (county boundaries have sometimes changed), and beside the Great Ridgeway (see 'Downland') are three principal sites. ***Wayland's Smithy*** is a Neolithic long barrow dating from around 3700 BCE. ***Dragon Hill*** *is a* natural chalk hill immediately below the ***Uffington White Horse***, a remarkable monument cut into the chalk downland. The name 'Dragon Hill' may derive from a legend that it was on its summit that Saint George, patron saint of England, slew the dragon.

Uluru: A large sandstone rock formation in Northern Territory, Australia, sacred to the Aboriginal people and known in colonial days as Ayers Rock.

West Kennet Long Barrow*:* A Neolithic tomb or barrow 3 km (one-and-a-half miles) south of Avebury in Wiltshire, England. It is close to ***Silbury Hill,*** a remarkable conical mound of a size comparable to the Giza pyramids whose purpose still puzzles archaeologists.

More Ideas

Here and in the colour photographs are some further ideas for spiritual pilgrimages that may inspire you:

- *A voyage to the stars....*
- *Alexandria and the rest of Egypt from a Christian perspective, as opposed to the Temples of the Nile and the Pyramids*
- *Alexandria, this time from a NeoPlatonic perspective, and the places associated with Pythagoras*
- *Arthurian Britain*
- *Assisi and Brother Francis*
- *Buddha and the shrines associated with him*
- *Bulgaria, as a gateway to Europe for early peoples and as the birthplace of Orpheus*
- *Callanish Stone Circle and other monuments on the Isle of Lewis*
- *Cathar France and Italy*
- *China's Holy Mountains (Buddhist, Taoist and Confucian)*
- *Cornish stone monuments*
- *Etruscan Italy*
- *Footsteps of great creative people – artists, musicians, poets*
- *Gobi Desert*
- *The Great Ridgeway, running from the Thames at Streatley to near Avebury, Wiltshire, one of the oldest roads in Europe*
- *Holy Land in the time of Jesus*
- *Jerusalem and the Crusades*
- *Joseph of Arimathaea*
- *Long-distance paths, exploring nature*
- *Mary, mother of Jesus, and Mary Magdalene and their travels*
- *Mecca*
- *Native American peoples, their sacred sites and their*

journeys and migrations
- *Ancient Greece*
- *Orthodox Greece*
- *PreChristian Celtic lands*
- *Quetzlcoatl*
- *Santiago di Compostela (the route of St James of Compostella)*

There are other ideas in the text itself, for instance Ephesus and Orkney; see Appendix 4. Ephesus also has connections with St John. Although Iona is spoken of as 'the isle of the blessed' by White Eagle, the appellation has been applied to almost every island off the west coast of Britain and Ireland, for instance the Isles of Scilly, off the toe of Cornwall.

A NOTE ON THE ILLUSTRATIONS

Colour Section

Page 1: 'Getting there' shows two walking situations in leafy woods, a cautionary tale about not taking too much baggage (of any sort!) and a view of endless mountains to remind us that there is plenty of room left on earth for the Masters! (Actual location: Sichuan, China, with the peak of Minya Kongka central in the distance; 'too much to carry' is actually carrying for a large group, Campcardos valley, Pyrenean France, 1994).

Pages 2 and 3, 'Standing Stones' are, clockwise from top left: ring of stones, Scottish west coast; Avebury; Waylands' Smithy; Stonehenge, and Callanish, Isle of Lewis. For locations see pp. 141–4.

Pages 4 and 5, 'To the Quiet Places', clockwise from top left: modern statue of St Francis surrounded by symbols of the world's religions – woods above Assisi; Sand Eels' Bay, Iona, looking across to Mull; star tile pattern from the Basilica di S. Francesco, Assisi; walkers in England's Peak District; Dorkang Monastery, Tibet; Iona Abbey, Scotland.

Page 6, 'The Labyrinth Experience': two images of the labyrinth on White Eagle land at Montgomery, Texas, are shown with the complex pattern of the Chartres labyrinth supermimposed.

Page 7, 'Cathar Country' shows, top to bottom: White Eagle party camped inside the château at Lordat, Ariège, 1994 (camping is no longer permitted: the area is an eagle sanctuary); the same party, enjoying the sunlight there; camping in a Pyrenean Cathar valley.

Page 8, 'Places in which to worship' shows the little Temple for World Peace in Sri Lanka actually created by Jenny Dent and friends; Jenny before the west front of Chartres Cathedral; a scene from the life of Gautama Buddha on the Peace Pavilion in London's Battersea Park; and the extraordinary 'lantern' above the crossing of nave and transepts in Ely Cathedral, Cambridgeshire, England.

Line Drawings in the Text

Rosemary Young has created a set of drawings, some of which are intended to be decorative and others informative. The reader may like to have a key to them, as follows.

p. 8   Tibetan Temple (1)
p. 11   Mountain scene (1)
p. 12   Riverbank scene
p. 13   Chalice
p. 20   Clay oil lamp, common in the ancient world
p. 25   Tibetan temple (2)
p. 47   Holy well, in the West Country of England

p. 54   Stone Figure, Easter Island, Pacific Ocean

p. 55   Temple at Edfu, ancient Egypt

p. 57   Labyrinth plan, rock carving at Tintagel,
         Cornwall

p. 64   High mountain and bird of prey

p. 68   Ruined château at Lordat, Ariège, France

p. 71   Machu Picchu, Peru

p. 72   Tibetan temple (3)

p. 82   Stonehenge, England

p. 92   Uluru, Central Australia

p. 96   Temple entrance

p. 116   Mountain (2)

p. 119   Dolmen from Cornwall, England

p. 123   Stone alignments at Carnac, in Brittany, France

p. 124   Bighorn Medicine Wheel, Wyoming, USA

p. 125   Bell Rock, Sedona, Arizona, USA

p. 127   Glastonbury Tor, England

p. 130   Egyptian pyramids

p. 135   Celtic Cross, like those found on Iona

p. 137   Avebury Stone Circle

p. 138   Lighted lamp

INDEX

Note: 'CS' = see picture in Colour Supplement

AFFIRMATIONS 64
Akasha, akashic 25–7
Albigenses, see Cathars
America 22, 60, 83, 117, 119, 124–5, 132, 145
Ancient Religions 21–2, 41
— Wisdom 9, 21n, 22, 112, 121, 128
Andes 71, 91, 114, 117, 119, 133
Ankh 56
Annapurna 69–70, 142
Antarctica 88–90
Apostles (rocks) 87–90
Ariège 65, 79–82, 142, 147, 148
Arthur, King 13–16, 18, 141, 143, 144
Assisi 107, 144, 146, CS
Astrological signs 62–3
Atlantic Ocean 89
Atlantis 14, 125
Aude 80
Australia 83, 88–94, 95–6, 99, 141, 142, 144, 148
Avebury 83–4, 98–101, 119, 121–2, 141, 144, 145, 146, CS

BERKSHIRE 74–7, 144
Bethlehem 43

Britain 10, 11, 13, 22, 41, 74, 76, 78, 82–8, 108, 109, 117, 119, 122, 126, 129, 144–5
Brodgar, Ring of 85–8
Brotherhood (quality) 15n, 17, 20n, 41, 62–3, 107, 135
Brotherhood (in spirit) 9, 13, 15, 16, 20, 24, 34, 37, 67, 69–70, 76–7, 113, 115, 120, 127 (see also Polaire Brotherhood)
Buddha, Buddhism 41–2, 47, 62, 141, 144, 145, 147, CS
Bunyan, John 39

CADER Idris 114, 141
Callanish 85–8, 144, 146, CS
Campcardos Valley 147, CS
Carnac 123, 141, 148
Castlerigg 108
Cathars or Albigenses 65–8, 79–82, 142, 143, 145, 147 CS
Cathedrals 52, 58, 84, 88, 94, 105–6, 117, 126, 128, 141, 147, CS
Celts 78, 100, 106, 145
Chartres Cathedral 58, 60, 94, 105, 141, 147, CS
China 145, 146, CS

Christ 17, 21n, 33, 66–7, 76,
    128n, 129
'Christian' (pilgrim) 39
Christianity 41, 67–8, 76, 84,
    86, 97, 106, 109, 126, 127,
    144, 145
Confucianism 145
Cooke, Grace 9–11, 65–8,
    74–77, 80
Cooke, Ivan 10, 74–7, 108–10
Cornwall 64, 104–5,119, 144,
    146, 149
Crystals 56, 70, 71
Cuzco 71

DENT, Jenny 10–11, 39, 69–75,
    94, 142, CS
Disciples, discipleship 37, 67,
    82, 88
Downland, English 36, 77–9,
    109, 141–2, 144
Dragon Hill 74–7, 143, 144
Dun–I 102, 142

EDFU 55–6, 141, 148
Egypt 14, 56, 119, 129–31
Elements 62–3
England 36, 74, 73, 83, 108,
    119, 141–4, 147–8
Ephesus, Turkey 97, 141, 146
Ether, etheric 10, 16, 22,
    25, 32–3, 50, 69–70, 75–7,
    109–10, 117, 120, 126, 133–4

FRANCE 65, 79–82, 119, 141,
    145, 146

GLASTONBURY 126–7, 142,
    148

Gospel(s) 67, 82
Great Barrier Reef 90–1, 142
Great Britain, see Britain
Great Ridgeway 142, 144
Greece 14, 146
Guide 9, 11, 42, 43, 49, 51, 56,
    58, 59, 59n, 68, 69, 97, 104,
    109, 111
Halls of Learning 27
Hayward, Colum 79
—, Geoffrey 77–9
—, Jeremy 82
—, Ylana 67–8, 107
Hermes Trismegistus 57
Himalaya 69–70, 71, 79, 91,
    114, 142
Hinduism 41–2
Hodgson, Joan 11, 63
Holy Grail, the 13, 18–20, 39,
    76, 136–8, 142
Holy Land 41, 81, 145
Horus 55, 141

ILLUMINATION 15n, 66, 76
Incas, the 71, 142
India 119, 131, 142
Indian Ocean 89
Indian, American 39
Iona 102–3,132–4, 142, 146,
    147, CS
Ireland 101, 114, 119, 143, 146
Isis 56
Islam 41–2

JERUSALEM 41–2, 145
Jesus 41, 43, 64, 67, 76, 81–2,
    88, 145 (see also 'Christ')
John the Baptist 67–8
Joseph of Arimathea 126

KNIGHTS (e.g. of the Grail, of the Rose Cross) 13–15, 39, 81

LABYRINTHS 57–62, 94–6, 148, CS
Languedoc 79–82
Light Bringer, The 11
Light in Britain, The 10, 11, 74, 108
Little Temple of World Peace, The 103, CS
Lordat 75, 79–82, 143, 148, CS

MACHAPUCHARE 69–70, 143
Machu Picchu 71, 143, 149
Maes Howe 87
Manor Place 64
Master(s), the 15, 20, 26, 53, 67, 70, 72, 91, 114
Master of the Star 70, 71
Mecca 42
Meditation 11, 20, 26, 29, 35–6, 49, 53, 59, 60, 95, 101–4, 136, 139
—, walking 61, 62–3 (see also 'walking')
Merlin 15
Minesta, see Grace Cooke
Montségur 66, 79–82, 143
Montagne de Tabe 81
Mosques 52
Mt Kailas 41
Mt Tabor 81–2
Mystery Schools 15, 21, 21n, 22, 112

NEPAL 69–70, 143
Newgrange 101, 143

ORKNEY Isles 85–8, 143, 148
Oxfordshire 74–7, 144

PACIFIC Ocean 89, 91
Pic de St-Barthélèmy 81, 143
Polaire Brotherhood 65–8, 79–82
Pyramid, Great 56–7, 130–1, 142
—s 56–7, 87, 130–2, 142, 145, 149
Pyrenees 63, 79–82, 143

QUEENSLAND 90–91, 142

ROMANS 78, 84, 141, 142
Rose Star Temple 20
Rosslyn Chapel 103, 105–6, 143, 143n
Round Table 13–14

SCOTLAND 96, 119, 132
Seeing and feeling 40, 46, 50, 74–5
Senses 29, 45, 49–50, 63, 73, 93, 110
Silbury Hill 83, 144
Sorbi, Jane 60
Southern Ocean 88–9
Sri Lanka 103
St Alban, St Albans 126–7
St Columba 102, 142
St Francis 47, 107, 145, 147, CS
St John 68, 70, 146
Star, stars 20, 43, 59, 62–3, 69–70, 74, 78, 104, 106, 115, 139–40
Star Action 103
Stonehenge 119–21, 143, CS

TAOISM 145
Teacher 8, 17, 52, 53–4, 57, 128
Temples 52, 54, 56, 83, 127–9,
   134–5
Thich Nhat Hanh 61, 62
Tibet 50, 55, 61, 69, 72–4, 100,
   142, 143, 147, 149
Tintagel 104–5, 144, 149
Tree of Light 62, 139

ULURU 87–94
Unstan, Tomb of (Orkney) 85–8

VARANASI, 41
Visualization 49, 51, 55-9, 63n,
   72

WALES 114, 119
Walking 28, 46, 56, 60, 61, 66,
   81-2, 94, 96, 147 (see also
   meditation)
White Eagle Lodge 10, 11, 77,
   88, 107
—, in America 60, 95
Wessex 141
West Kennet Long Barrow
   83–5, 144
White Brotherhood 24, 37,
   69–70, 77
Wiltshire 122, 141–4, 145
'Wingless flight' 49–51
Wisdom in the Stars 11, 63

NOTES

Two White Eagle books to read after this one

WALKING WITH THE ANGELS

White Eagle's teaching gives insights into the entire angelic kingdom, from the guardian angels who trigger the miracles in our lives to the great beings who are masters of the rays of creation. He speaks of the angels of creativity with whom we may work, and the angels operating in the rhythms of nature with whom we may find harmony.

This book, which contains commentary by Anna Hayward, can enhance the life of any reader who learns through it to walk a path of co-operation and creativity with the angels.

Matt-laminated flapped paperback,
132 +xii pp, 21.6 x 13.8 cm
ISBN 978-0-85487-109-4

EARTH HEALER

A guide to drawing on spiritual consciousness as a healing tool for planet earth. White Eagle's teaching has been changing lives for over seventy years, but not for years has there been quite as important or as timely a collection of his teaching as this one. It represents a blue-print for our individual and collective transformation.

White Eagle insists that 'saving the planet' need not be a process of fear and reaction, but one of attunement to the natural process of evolution in human awareness. Our very thoughts influence the thoughts of others; our own attention to beauty actually creates beauty. Real love of nature attacks wastefulness; trust in the natural processes of life removes the fears about life and death that create greed and selfishness. Humanity can and will change.

The book also celebrates the harmony of the natural world through the photographs of Bruce Clarke, whose sensitive eye finds beauty in every conceivable natural-world situation.

96pp, paperback, 20 x 20 cm
ISBN 978-0-85487-214-5

THE WHITE EAGLE LODGE
www.whiteagle.org

The White Eagle Lodge is based on the profound yet gentle philosophy of White Eagle. Through his teaching we receive encouragement on a path of love, tolerance and service towards all life: a path which offers the development of inner peace and the awareness of our eternal, spiritual nature.

There are many groups throughout the world, and they can be found by contacting the main centres given below. These centres offer services of healing, meditation, spiritual unfoldment and retreats.

White Eagle's teaching is offered in the printed and electronic books of the White Eagle Publishing Trust (www.whiteaglepublishing.org), alongside CDs and other publications. Books currently in print are listed opposite the title page of this volume.

Readers wishing to know more of the work of the White Eagle Lodge should check the website above or contact The White Eagle Lodge, New Lands, Brewells Lane, Liss, Hampshire GU33 7HY.

In the Americas, please write to
The Church of the White Eagle Lodge
P. O. Box 930, Montgomery, Texas 77356
(tel. 936-597 5757; www.whiteaglelodge.org;
in *Canada*, use www.whiteagle.ca)
and in *Australasia* please write to
The White Eagle Lodge (Australasia)
P. O. Box 225, Maleny, Queensland 4552
(tel. 07-5494 4397; www.whiteaglelodge.org.au).

If using *email*, contact us via
enquiries@whiteagle.org (worldwide)
sjrc@whiteagle.org (Americas)
enquiries@whiteeaglelodge.org.au (Australasia)